The last years of R.L.S.

were spent living and writing
among the Pacific islands

Requiem.

Under the wide and starry sky,
Dig the grave and let me lie.
Glad did I live and gladly die
    And I laid me down with a will.

Here may the winds about me blow;
Here the clouds may come and go;
Here shall be rest for evermo,
    And the heart for aye shall be still

This be the verse you grave for me:
Here he lies where he longed to be;
Home is the sailor, home from sea,
    And the hunter home from the hill

HOME FROM THE SEA
Robert Louis Stevenson in Samoa

BY

RICHARD A. BERMANN

TRANSLATED BY

ELIZABETH REYNOLDS HAPGOOD

MUTUAL PUBLISHING PAPERBACK SERIES
TALES OF THE PACIFIC
HONOLULU • HAWAII

Cover design by Momi Cazimero

Cover photo courtesy of the Baker-Van Dyke Collection

Printed in Australia by The Book Printer, Victoria

For a complete listing of other books in the "Tales
of the Pacific" series and ordering information,
write to:

Mutual Publishing Company
2055 N. King Street
Honolulu, Hawaii 96819

Phone: (808) 924-7732

**THIS BOOK CONTAINS THE COMPLETE TEXT
OF THE ORIGINAL HARDBOUND EDITION**

PREFACE

MY book is the story of the two last years of Robert Louis Stevenson's life. It is told without ornament, without any additional invention. I have used all sources available to me, especially Stevenson's letters, which I have sometimes repeated word for word; his articles which he sent from Samoa to the London *Times* and other periodicals; the biographies which appeared after his death, notably the book by his cousin, Sir Graham Balfour, who lived with the Stevensons at Vailima. Then there are the letters of his mother, and especially the many articles and books in which his stepchildren, Isobel Strong (later Mrs. Field) and Lloyd Osbourne described their life with R. L. S. Lloyd Osbourne's biographical sketches in the "Tusitala Edition" of Stevenson's works are the most beautiful things which have been written about this lovable and complex man.

I have drawn my material from all these sources and many others. I have attempted to describe the unique figure of the dying Stevenson without deviating by as much as a hair's breadth from the actual biographical data; not even to the extent of changing a date. There is perhaps one single exception, and this I feel I can justify. I have moved the date of the last visit of King Malietoa Laupepa to

Vailima, and the psychologically interesting incident which occurred then, to the year 1893, whereas Graham Balfour holds that the episode belongs in 1894. But none of Stevenson's letters for 1894 which have so far been published mention this very important visit from the King, whereas a letter written in April, 1893, could easily be interpreted to imply that the King of the Samoans had, at a critical moment, sought out the great friend of his people, "Tusitala," the Teller of Tales.

Although I have been actuated by loyalty to biographical data, I do not present this book as a biography, but rather I hope to see it read as an exotic tale whose hero is the man Robert Louis Stevenson rather than the famous author. The idea of writing this book came to me in 1925 as I stood before Stevenson's grave on the crest of Mt. Vaea. For I have visited Samoa and Vailima, I have talked to Samoans who knew Tusitala, and I can judge what he was to them and what they meant to him.

R. A. B.

CONTENTS

CHAPTER I

"MY NAME IS MR. DUMBLEY"

IN the early days of the year 1893 a dark spirit sped like a storm over the South Seas: the whites called it influenza; the natives knew it only as the foreign sickness. For it was an illness of the foreign white people; in their faraway countries they had known it for a long time, and in their variously infected blood they had long since developed immunities. But before the coming of the whites the Polynesians had known nothing of diseases and were quite defenceless before them; for them a measles epidemic was as deadly as the plague, and the grippe as dangerous as cholera.

It was not without reason that the Samoans, when they saw the first white "Papalangi" sail into their harbours, prayed to the ancient deities of the island: "Drive these sailing gods away from here, lest they come and bring us sickness and death!"

The influenza epidemic paralyzed the whole life of Apia, the harbour town, and soon spread to the Vailima plantation; Robert Louis Stevenson's new house looked like a hospital. In the beautiful great hall, of which he was so

3

proud, places had been improvised for the sick, and mattresses laid on the ground with mosquito netting hung over them. There they lay, Talolo, Sosimo, Jopu, Misifolo and the other nut-brown men who had been cheerful servants in the house, and workers on the plantation; and they groaned piteously, feeling themselves to be already as good as dead and buried. For the Polynesian Kanaka makes no effort to struggle against this mysterious and foreign enchantment, sickness. He gives himself up the minute he is attacked by it.

All work on the plantation ceased. Tropical weeds sprang up triumphantly among the young coco palms. Everything was topsy-turvy in the house which heretofore had been so comfortably regulated.

On the morning of January 16, Isobel Strong entered her stepfather's bedroom. It was usual that he should be awake at dawn; one of the Samoan servants brought him a cup of tea, whereupon Stevenson started immediately to work lying in bed. That is to say, he sat, rather than lay, on his Spartan couch. He would not have any mattress on his bed; he had only some finely woven Samoan mats under him. But behind him he had an elaborate back rest which his friend, Sir Percy Shelley, a son of the poet, had given him. Thus he sat, long before the rest of the household was awake, with his portfolio propped against his drawn-up knees, making notes on the chapters he would dictate, in the course of the morning, to his stepdaughter secretary.

As soon as Isobel came into the room, notebook in hand, she realized that something was wrong for Louis lay there so stiffly. He was rather fantastically garbed even in bed, with a scarlet scarf wrapped around his thin body, which was encased in a blue and white Japanese kimono. His long, finely moulded face, usually boyish in spite of the soft moustache, or impish, or both, was pale today under its tan. His wonderful brown eyes shone brighter than usual. He smiled, as always, when Isobel came to his room in the morning, but his usual merry greeting did not cross his tightly closed lips; instead, he reached out a waxen pale hand and pointed to a slate which lay beside his bed. Isobel took the slate and read: "Allow me to introduce myself: my name is Dumbley."

While Isobel read his message, R. L. S. grinned rather mischievously. But a drop of blood, which oozed slowly through his closed lips and ran down his chin, betrayed the reason why Louis had introduced himself as Dumbley; he was having a hemorrhage. When this happened he dared not speak; in this way he was sometimes able to hold back the flow of blood from his sick lungs.

Man is a strange creature, full of mysterious impulses. Isobel Strong was certainly deeply frightened. Yet her first clear thought was not one of concern for the beloved invalid. It was for the novel he was working on. It was not his stepdaughter, but his zealous secretary who thought: "Too bad! He won't be able to dictate today and we were getting along so well with the St. Ives story."

5

Then suddenly all the novels in the world shrank into nothingness. "Oh Lou, poor Lou!"

She wiped the blood from his chin, fixed him more comfortably in his bed and ran to arouse her mother.

In the twelve years of her marriage with the invalid, Fanny Stevenson had been through many days like this one, when spasms threatened to destroy the tender vessel which was R. L. S. Once in Hyères, on the Mediterranean, his trembling hand had written this line for her: "Do not be afraid! If this is death, it is an easy death!"

She had laughingly pretended that that was one of his jokes. Hundreds of times, during those dozen years, the little American woman had forced a smile on her dark face as she entered the room with a light, carefree, friendly remark on her trembling lips, much as an older brother comes to the sickbed of a beloved little boy. Then she calmly and confidently took possession of the patient, for on these occasions he belonged entirely to her. Wilful as he was, he capitulated completely to her gentle tyranny.

Now she smiled at him again as she took charge. And he smiled back at her, but not as he had done earlier to her daughter. Then he had grinned with amusement—though he might be dying—and a little ironically. Now his smile was rather guilty; yes, he hung his head between his shoulders as though he were afraid he might be scolded because he was ill.

Fanny took the situation into her firm little hands with all

6

of her accustomed capability. Before she had gone to the sickroom, after Isobel's first alarm, she had already dispatched her son Lloyd to the city to get the doctor.

Now there were a thousand things to do and to arrange. The grippe had disorganized the house; even the cook Talolo was sick in bed, and Fanny had to cook for everyone; which, incidentally, she loved to do. She was needed in the kitchen, and in the hall where the sick servants were groaning and fussing; yet she found time to sit quietly on the foot of Louis' bed and chat calmly.

She was small and doll-like, but not of delicate proportions; in fact, she was rather solidly built. Her face was so dark that, although she was descended from Hollanders, she was often taken for a mulatto; she wore large gold rings in her ears. She was dressed in the holoku apron of the native women and her feet were, as always when indoors, bare.

She was ten years older than R. L. S., and the difference was apparent. Yet, as she sat on the edge of his bed, she seemed to radiate great strength and energy.

"It is only the grippe," said Fanny to her husband. "How could it have missed you when half the house is down with it?"

Then she proceeded to talk about household affairs, not in a tone of complaint, but merely to distract the nervous patient until the doctor arrived. She told about the wild goings on earlier in the morning out in the hall when an emaciated youth, by the name of Misifolo, had begun to scream in a

7

delirium of fever, and about how, at the climax of excitement and confusion, Simele had suddenly appeared with a pail of water and a broom and, since no one else was around, had proceeded to wash up one patient after another.

Henry Simele was the young chieftain of Savaii Island who acted as principal overseer of the native workers on the Vailima plantation; he was so highborn that the others dared not even address him in Samoan, but were obliged to use a special language, reserved for intercourse with high chiefs.

"And now His Highness is going around like a chambermaid," said Fanny, "not paying any attention to the ancient gods of his ancestors. I know, of course, he is not doing it to please me, Louis, but for your sake. They do nothing because you order them or pay them to do it, but they will do anything in their power out of loyalty or for love. . . ."

I wonder what he is looking at, thought Fanny, as she rippled on. The "flying cloud," for which the Samoans had named her Aolele, passed quickly over her face and disappeared, leaving a smile in its place. (He is looking out of the window, to the top of that mountain and thinking, "That is where they will bury me!")

She drew a deep breath and said, "You know, I think I hear horses in front of the house. Can Lloyd be back already with the doctor?"

Whenever anything happened to his stepfather, and that was often, young Lloyd Osbourne rode into town himself to fetch the doctor, because the native servants, for all their devotion to Tusitala, were capable of loitering for several hours along the way. On these days when he galloped the three miles to Apia in furious haste, the narrow trail through the dense growth of the primeval forest seemed so different! At other times, on carefree days, the play of light and shade in the tropical luxuriance fascinated him. Today there was something threatening about it: the dark boughs seemed to snatch at him, the roots and the lianas writhed like venomous snakes; the song of the birds mocked him, then there was a sudden ominous silence that clutched at his throat. So he rode today, a tall overgrown youth, serious beyond his twenty-five years. He wore glasses, and on his head was an American cowboy hat, against which the branches of the trees kept brushing.

The road was very poor—full of holes and rough places. One had to be extremely careful; yet Lloyd Osbourne never forgot for a second the thought that was tormenting him: if he should die this time? if he should die? What if he should die, whispered another voice, his conscience, before everything has been talked out and cleared up between us? Why am I so painfully shy, so tongue-tied with him?

In his anguish, as it happens with a drowning man, Lloyd Osbourne saw in a flash all the pictures of his past. There was that memorable day in the forest of Fontainebleau—how long ago? Was it sixteen, seventeen years? He, Lloyd Osbourne, was a boy of eight then, and he was not called Lloyd, but Sam, for his father, Sam Osbourne. His mother was married then to that blond bearded giant, a gold miner, bear hunter, adventurer; but she could not stand life with him in California, so she had taken her three children and run away to Europe, thinking she would study art in Paris with Belle, and they would both become famous painters. In Paris, the youngest of the children, Harvey, a little blond angel whom Sam adored, was taken suddenly ill and died. The family, quite overwhelmed by the shock, had sought seclusion in the forest. They lived in Grez, in a pension frequented by artists of the Barbizon school. On that particular day the guests of the boardinghouse were all seated at a long table: the wild young painters, Sam's mother, his half-grown sister Isobel and he himself. Suddenly, in the midst of their meal, a stranger stepped through the open window, a young man with long hair falling to the shoulders of his velvet jacket. The painters raised a great commotion: "Stevenson! Why, it really is Stevenson!" A man by this name had been expected at the pension, and for several days the painters had talked about this miraculous being; about how talented, how brilliant, how gay and eccentric he was, with the result that the boy had formed a strong antipathy to him. Now the man stood in the room and bowed with consciously exaggerated gallantry to the two American ladies. From his corner little Sam glowered at him; he was determined not even to speak to him.

10

Suddenly Mr. Stevenson looked his way and smiled at him with beaming eyes. The cross little boy began positively to melt under the warmth of the stranger's smile. That afternoon saw them already down on all fours together in a corner of the dining room, contentedly playing a marvellous new game that the stranger had invented with Sam's lead soldiers.

Another memory was of the old Spanish town of Monterey in California, in the autumn of 1879. "Uncle Luly," who was by then adored by Sam and worshipped as a hero, had suddenly turned up in California. He was even thinner than the ten-year-old boy had remembered him; his eyes glowed more intensely but rather strangely; his velvet jacket was very shabby and flapped around Uncle Luly's body. To the boy he was still the same happy and fascinating playmate. The grown-up Lloyd Osbourne knew now what little Sam had not known at the time: that Stevenson, because he had no money, had come to New York in a tramp ship; that he had crossed the continent in a train intended for poor immigrants; that he was already ill when he reached California; that he had suffered there from lack of food and thereby given all but the last blow to his already delicate health. Those eyes were brilliant with fever; that kind uncle, who brought him chocolate, had too little to eat himself, and he was working in a newspaper office for two dollars a week.

What could Sam know? To him it was quite natural that Uncle Luly had travelled all the way to California to play with him again. That was wonderful. They could take walks together through the sleepy, sun-drenched streets of the old Spanish town, between houses of adobe brick, or out along the gleaming ocean beach, and he could tell him stories. No one could tell stories like this beloved uncle. Stories? Why, you were right in it yourself, as an Indian chief or a pirate. These stories still stuck vaguely in his memory like shafts of sunlight breaking through a fog.

But there was one picture from those days that stood out fearfully clear and stark. It was of his father, Samuel Osbourne, the gold miner. He was tall, robust, and had a pointed blond beard. He suddenly appeared and no one knew where he had come from. He stood in his mother's room, while Sam was in the next room doing his homework for school. Little Sam of those days liked big Sam's voice; he liked his father whom he so seldom saw. He was quite different from Uncle Luly. He was not so radiantly gay, not so delicate and thin; but powerfully built, a bear hunter, a man who really had shot Indians; he carried a revolver on his hip, and from his watch chain dangled a gold nugget he had found himself.

The voices next door grew louder. His father and mother were quarrelling. Suddenly, after a tearful silence, he heard his mother say, in an unforgettably tragic tone, "Oh, Sam, please forgive me!"

The next day, during their walk together, Robert Louis Stevenson was unusually silent. Then he turned to the boy

12

and told him quite frankly that his mother was going to get a divorce from Samuel Osbourne. "And I have something else to tell you, Sam. I do not know what you will say to it, but I hope it will make you happy: I am going to marry your mother."

Grown-up Lloyd Osbourne remembered that he had stood there quite stunned for a while. Then, without saying a word, he had pushed his cold little fist into the feverishly hot hand of his emaciated companion.

A year later, Lloyd Osbourne recalled, it was a rainy summer in the Scottish Highlands. All around the tiny house, which belonged to a Mrs. McGregor, high on the cliffs above Pitlochry, bloomed the heather; the smell of it still lingered in his memory. In this house the Stevensons lived. Now they were Mr. and Mrs. Stevenson; only the boy still carried the name of Osbourne, but they called him by his second name, Lloyd, and not Sam any more.

Oh, those rainy days in the Scottish Highlands! His memory was that the rain never ceased. Sam-Lloyd, who was on his vacation, would have been bored if he had not been given an inexpensive but exciting box of paints. There he sat in a corner of the room, a serious little fellow, busily smearing colours on one sheet after another, while outside it poured. The older boy, his playmate, otherwise known as Robert Louis Stevenson, had theoretically no time to play with Lloyd. He was trying for a professorship at the University of Edinburgh—this was something substantial at last, something to bring in money—and for that reason he had to study Scottish Constitutional History. In practice, however, he naturally spent all of his days sitting on the floor with the schoolboy and playing with paints.

Now he borrows the colours and the brush for a minute to paint something himself on a sheet of paper. Look, Lloyd, today we are going to paint something wonderful. Here is a map—of course it is an island—don't you see all the blue water I am painting around it? That point, which juts out into the water, is a cape. In this dent on the shore line there is a harbour, and a ship is anchored there. What kind of ship? Wait a bit. It is a brig. No, it is the schooner *Hispaniola*, two hundred tons, out of Bristol. Of course there are cannon aboard; how could you fight sea robbers without them? But, Sam, I mean Lloyd, of course there are adventurers aboard, keen to hunt for treasure; yes, indeed, buried pirate treasure. Adventurers? Adventurers are not necessarily all criminals; there are some fine fellows among them. Take Jim, for example, the cabin boy on the *Hispaniola;* he is terribly brave and noble. . . .

Grown-up Lloyd Osbourne could still see that scene distinctly, with Louis kneeling on the floor drawing and painting everything that belonged to a high-class pirate island: the Island mountains, the spring, the cave, the spot with the skeleton and that other spot where the chest with the doubloons was buried.

14

When this marvellous map was finished, Louis wrote on it in his scrawny hand:

TREASURE ISLAND

Then he grew pensive and stopped playing, or, if you will, he began to play in earnest; for he took his notebook and wrote: "The Old Buccaneer," "The Black Spot," "The Sea-Chest," as chapter headings for the story he was planning.

"What shall we call our story?" asked the little boy with burning cheeks.

"I do not know yet," said his big playmate, and coughed, for he had caught another cold. "Perhaps *The Sea Cook,* because you know the *Hispaniola* has a one-legged sailor for a cook. He is a terrible scoundrel; a former pirate. Or, how do you like the title, *Treasure Island?*"

The grown-up young man, who was once the little boy to whom Robert Louis Stevenson first told the story of *Treasure Island,* now saw another little house, this time in the Swiss mountains in winter. It was Davos-Platz. Stevenson was still unknown and very poor, for the extraordinary success of *Treasure Island* was still in the future. During that winter he was sick enough and desperate enough to die. He was often incapable of any concentration or serious work. So he helped Lloyd, the schoolboy, with his highly important and lucrative business: a little child's printing press which published programs for the concerts in the fashionable Hotel Belvédère, where wealthy guests stayed to try to cure their sick lungs.

When Lloyd Osbourne printed one of these programs, he proudly set on the title page: "Published by the Davos Press, Samuel Lloyd Osbourne, proprietor." Nor was this the whole of the young publisher's ambitious undertaking. He also printed real books; yes, even illustrated books. The illustrations were provided by a gifted apprentice who helped the proprietor; his name was Stevenson. He made all kinds of pictures, woodcuts. There was, for example, a pirate with a sabre, and an apothecary with a silk hat. The printer's apprentice also wrote highly moral tales to go with the pictures, and amusingly rhymed verses. The chief printer set them up, without too great a regard for spelling, and then peddled them from house to house.

The lean young man galloping through the virgin forest of Samoa had to laugh, in spite of his choking anxiety, as he thought of the late "Davos Press." Those childish booklets, printed on a toy press and offered in the Davos hotels, mostly without success, for the price of sixpence, were sought after now by Stevenson's admirers through the length and breadth of the entire world. They were not worth their weight in gold, because they were so light they could not weigh down the golden sovereigns now paid for them.

He must not die! thought the lonely rider through the tropical forest, as he spurred his horse. There was no reason why he must die this time; these hemorrhages had happened often and today's did not seem so bad.

But, if——

If his stepfather should die!

No, young Lloyd Osbourne could not call him that. Louis was Louis. Once his playmate. Later his comrade during that long, difficult and often dangerous cruise through the barbaric archipelagoes of the South Seas. Playmate, comrade, friend—and now his chief and employer, for Lloyd managed the plantation, and he was also his collaborator. Lloyd Osbourne's real profession was writing, and his yet young and unknown name had already figured on the title page of a book next to the world-famous name of Stevenson: *The Wrecker*, A Novel by Robert Louis Stevenson and Lloyd Osbourne.

Friend, benefactor, everything. But father? Lloyd Osbourne did not know it, but deep down in his heart a tall, blond, powerful gold miner and bear hunter, by the name of Sam, fought against this ailing, delicate, proud, glamorous creature; against this man who could tell a boy a story like *Treasure Island*, but who could never be a father to him.

Overcome by a bewildering mixture of emotions, of fear, sense of guilt, opposition to and tender love for the invalid, Lloyd Osbourne spurred his horse on.

For God's sake, if only the doctor is in!

Dr. Funk, the German doctor of the little colonial town of Apia, with his parted beard looked like Admiral von

Tirpitz. He did not take the report of the happenings at Vailima very tragically. He was hard pressed by the influenza epidemic, and would probably not have ridden out there immediately had it not been a question of the author Stevenson. Particularly as this gentleman, from the political point of view, was rather a disturbing element. At this moment he was not in too high favour with the Imperial German Consulate, but as a private individual he enjoyed the greatest esteem in the colony; his material standing was undoubtedly high, and when it came to paying doctor's bills, no matter what they said of his Scottish countrymen, he was generous.

"Of course I shall ride out with you, Herr Osbourne! Just one moment while I get my bag. He has probably picked up an infection, your poor stepfather, and it would be a miracle if he didn't. . . . Now where is that ergotin? Where, in the devil's name, is the ergotin! I must take a small bottle of ergotin along."

It was a hard, laborious ride out to Vailima, and Dr. Funk's resemblance was really to an admiral, not a cavalry general.

"I am afraid, my dear Mr. Osbourne, that we cannot entirely cure your stepfather even in our famous South Seas climate. But there is no reason why he should not live for a number of years. I have known tubercular people who, with a little care, and not too much work, and especially with no political excitements . . ."

At the patient's bedside Funk, having pulled a properly

18

dignified doctor's face, tested Stevenson's pulse and temperature, listened to his heart and lungs, and then went down, none the wiser, to the hall to look at the sick natives. Soon you could hear Misifolo's screams all the way to the master's bedroom. That swarthy youth, who had not lived very long as yet among these extraordinary white people, had a horror of the Papalangi medicine man with two pairs of eyes, who held you in a very suspicious manner by the wrist and tried to force you to drink a bitter magic potion.

Stevenson was still condemned to silence and looked at his resolute wife, who sat beside him, the embodiment of the genius of nursing.

"Misifolo makes too much fuss," said Fanny. "He gets all the others excited. I think we shall have to send him away from the house because he is really too savage still. Let's play a game of solitaire!"

Whenever Fanny Stevenson had to keep this most sensitive of creatures quietly in bed, she played a special kind of solitaire with him, which she had learned once upon a time from the nihilist, Prince Kropotkin, whom the Stevensons had met during his exile. Fanny was not bad as a solitaire player, but R. L. S. understood the complications of the game far better than she. As he was not allowed to speak, he watched her in silence; but whenever she put up a card which, according to his ideas, ought not to have been played yet, he winked and kept winking until she took it back. Although they never put their feelings on this subject into words, there was a tacit understanding between them that the result of the solitaire would be a good or a bad omen; if it came out, everything would go well and the danger would be over. Louis, who was as excited as a boy by any game, and who was always keyed up by anything he was doing, watched closely and gave Fanny yeoman assistance in difficult situations; and, thanks to him, they eventually came to a successful conclusion. Strangely enough, Fanny Stevenson, who believed in portents, and would have been deeply depressed at this moment by a bad omen, was annoyed, although she would not have admitted it, that the game was won by the helpless invalid, and not by her.

She got up.

"Now, my darling, you must be good and stay alone for an hour, and try to get some sleep. You heard the doctor say you mustn't have too much company!"

And she gathered up the cards.

Suddenly left alone, Stevenson twisted himself around in his bed until he could look out of the window. The bed was so placed that from it he could see the wooded crest of Mt. Vaea; yet this was something that was never mentioned in Vailima. Everyone in the household knew that one day R. L. S. would be buried on the little plateau on top of Mt. Vaea. It was like Louis to flirt stubbornly with this mountain of destiny, and like his household to ignore the existence of the mountaintop just as stubbornly; not one of them, save Louis of the sick lungs, had ever been up there. Lloyd Osbourne, the official head of the workmen on the plantation, had over and over again received orders from his stepfather to cut a passable trail to the top of Mt. Vaea, and he had silently and stubbornly left the orders unfulfilled. Now that Fanny had left him so abruptly, Louis immediately took his revenge on her as a resentful little boy might do on his mother; he looked over to the mountain, trying to recall distinctly the setting of his future burial place. He thought of the verses he had long since prepared for his headstone:

> "Under the wide and starry sky,
> Dig the grave and let me lie.
> Glad did I live and gladly die." . . .

Now the magic power of the will to live had already completely transformed the sick man's thoughts. Although his spiritual eye might still rest on those exalted, but perhaps not altogether true, words, "Glad did I live and gladly die," still his longing, given wings by his impulse to live, had flown after his hope, his life; and instead of landing atop the wild crest of the Samoan mountain Vaea, had made a beeline for another mountain, in the midst of his native town of Edinburgh. In looking for some plausible reason for this altered destination, he found it instantly in the fictitious person of a certain Vicomte Anne de Keroual St. Ives, the romantic hero of the novel R. L. S. was working on at the moment. St. Ives was a hero after the heart of this Scottish writer with French leanings: a soldier of Napoleon, a prisoner of war in the camp on the precipitous heights of the Castle Rock in Edinburgh. It is difficult to escape if one is imprisoned there, or when one is buried on the crest of Mt. Vaea under the wide and starry sky. . . .

But, of course, he will escape, this slender young Frenchman, St. Ives, and in the end he will win his Scottish sweetheart, and will even become a Scot; it will, oh, it must, all end happily as a real story of adventure should. It shall end happily! cries Robert Louis Stevenson, pressing back the fatal stream of blood that threatens to gush forth. One can even escape, in the end, from the top of a mountain, if one has the courage to find the way. . . .

The invalid, who but now was home in Edinburgh, found himself back again in his little room in Vailima, and he wrinkled his brow, because he must turn his thoughts once more to the trail leading to the top of Mt. Vaea. The day would come when a large, heavy burden must be carried up there, through thickets of underbrush, over the slippery layers of lava. . . .

For an instant his thoughts centered again on his future burial. He had a clear vision of every detail, and again he saw them building the trail through the virgin forest; but now it had changed to the jungle of Tahiti, where he was planning to lay the South Sea novel, *Sophia Scarlet*. First he wanted to finish *Ebb Tide* and *St. Ives,* then do *Sophia Scarlet.* After that, he wished to work on a fascinating subject, the story about Stevenson's favourite character, in which that charming and evil Master of Ballantrae would appear again, *The Young Chevalier*. Yes, and there was, of course, that story of stories, the magnum opus that R. L. S. wanted to achieve, *Weir of Hermiston*. This great novel was to picture in immortal form, not the South Seas, but the strange, uncouth fascination of Scotland, land of mists.

If I succeed, R. L. S. thought suddenly, in dictating, one after another, all these stories I have planned and which are all ready in my head; if I have no interruption, what royalties could I count on in the next two years, including payments for serial rights?

And his thoughts, which had been flitting back and forth between Vaea, the mountain of destiny, and Castle Rock in his native Edinburgh, finally settled down on a column of figures. It had always come to this, for no matter how free and romantic a life this invalid appeared to lead, he must earn money with his writing. Now, more than ever. He calculated: How many people are dependent on me? Not my mother; whether she lives at home in Scotland or here in Vailima, she has my father's money. But Fanny, Lloyd, Isobel—Isobel's husband, Joe Strong, no longer earns any money as a painter; he just sits around on the plantation. He will never amount to anything; that marriage is obviously going on the rocks, and soon. I shall have to go on supporting her son, Austin Strong; I already pay for his tuition in a school in San Francisco. So much for the family.

23

Then there is the "Clan Tusitala," the household and the plantation workers. There are a dozen or two of them according to the operations carried on. It is fine, though, that out here on the rim of the world, I hold a semibarbaric court, and have retainers, just like any Scottish chieftain in the Highlands at home, only it costs money; and the plantation does not produce anything substantial. . . .

Everything costs money—Tusitala's house gleaming in the tropical sun; the garden where Fanny makes a thousand expensive experiments; the swarm of garlanded Samoan retainers who, on Sundays, put on the Vailima livery, kilts of Stuart plaid, over their tattooed legs; the horse Lloyd rides on as he bosses the workers on the plantation; the pretty gilt rings Isobel gives to the Samoan girls—all cost money. It costs money even to enjoy the elegiac pleasure of possessing a future burial place on a cloud-wreathed crest of an exotic mountain in the South Seas, under the wide and starry sky. . . .

It costs money which must be earned. Thank God, the Stevenson vogue is at its height, editions are multiplying. But the expenses are running them a close race. The family is not yet provided for against the day, when . . .

There is no other way; another story must be dictated, and then another—Scottish novels, South Sea stories, historical novels, modern romances. Not to mention journalistic work and a crushing amount of correspondence. How many embryonic novels have we on hand at present? Four? Five?

With *Weir of Hermiston* there are five. But *Weir* cannot be automatically counted in with the others. Oh, if only he could get rid of the whole lot—all this stuff to amuse children—and have the peace to work slowly and carefully, as one should, on this roughhewn, rain-soaked Scottish novel, fragrant with the smell of heather and mountain streams, the story of the "hanging judge," Weir of Hermiston, Lord Justice-Clerk of Scotland.

The sick man, who could see from his bed the top of Mt. Vaea, suddenly clutched his throat with both hands, as though to press back the blood that kept rising to his mouth to choke him. Not that, not yet, not until *Weir of Hermiston* has been quietly brought to fruition, a lasting masterpiece!

When the appointed hour of rest was over, the various members of the family came in, one at a time, to spend a little while with R. L. S. First Lloyd made a short visit to the patient; in a tone of forced gayety he told an anecdote about Simele and their cook, Talolo. But the real conversation between Lloyd and "Mr. Dumbley" was carried on by their eyes; to put it into words it would read:

"Why have you not had that trail built to the top of the mountain, Lloyd?"

"Because I don't want to. Do you hear? I won't do it, Louis!"

Lloyd went away, but he knew that the sick man's eyes

would fly again to the window and to the dark outline of the mountain.

The place was boiling with household and hospital activities, so the energetic Fanny could only dash into the bedroom for a few moments, a smile on her dark face, to say a few gay words of command and then go out, leaving the chair by the patient's bed to her daughter Belle for the long afternoon hours; Fanny had to cook supper and take care of the influenza patients in the hall. Belle had the job of entertaining but not exciting Louis. He must under no circumstances say a single word and might write only what was absolutely necessary.

First of all, Isobel smoothed out his pillows and placed some bright red hibiscus blossoms on the table by the bed. She always felt the need of decorating and beautifying everything around her. That is why the Samoans, who are good observers, gave her the name, Teuila, the adorner.

Isobel Strong was only eight years her stepfather's junior, and she mothered him a little the way her mother did. Since Belle had come back to live with her mother, R.L.S., that sensitive plant, had thriven on the love and also on the determined will of these two energetic women.

When Belle came to see him this time, he wrote on the slate: "Mr. Dumbley is still dumb. The devil take it; it is such a nuisance!"

While she was reading it, he hung his head a little guiltily, as though he were afraid of the wrath of his strict secretary, because he could not dictate his usual quota today. Today there could be no talk of that; no talk of talk. But Belle had an inspiration. She took up his joke.

"Mr. Dumbley, just how dumb are you even if you cannot speak without opening your mouth? Don't you know that people can talk with their hands?"

Isobel Strong, like her mother, possessed a talent for a thousand little arts. Somewhere she had picked up the deaf and dumb alphabet! That was the very sort of thing for R. L. S.; his eyes positively glowed. In an instant he had forgotten everything else, his hemorrhage, the ominous crest of Mt. Vaea, all his cares, all his longings, all literature— At this moment there was nothing of any importance in the whole wide world, from the North Sea to the South Seas, except this new game. He applied himself feverishly to the task of mastering the deaf and dumb alphabet. This is how you hold your fingers to form the letter A. That is easy, but other letters are more difficult. In no time at all R. L. S. knew the language of the dumb better than his teacher. He played with it all afternoon and could not get enough of it. His brown fingers flew through the air, forming A,B,C; then whole words and finally sentences. Now it was Belle's turn to follow with difficulty.

The next day a play was given in the sickroom of Robert Louis Stevenson, the like of which had probably never been seen before; R. L. S. dictated his new novel, *St. Ives,* to his secretary with his fingers, in the language of the deaf and

27

dumb. As he dictated five solid pages of powerfully clear and ironically subtle text, Mr. Dumbley's eyes looked out of the window once more to the fateful mountain-top, but this time they were full of joy and triumph.

A week later the grippe had been conquered, two little hemorrhages had come and gone and Robert Louis Stevenson, no longer Mr. Dumbley, could speak again like any healthy person. The first thing he dictated out loud was a letter to his best friend in London, Professor Sidney Colvin, a curator at the British Museum.

Speaking of his new novel, an impish smile came over his face as he dictated to Isobel:

"The Amanuensis has her head quite turned and believes herself to be the author of this novel . . . the creature—"

After the word "creature" the secretary put an undictated exclamation point.

"—the creature has not been wholly useless. . . . I propose to foster her vanity by a little commemoration gift! The name of the hero is Anne de St. Yves; . . . It is my idea to get a ring made which shall either represent *Anne* or A.S.Y. A., of course, would be Amethyst and S. Sapphire. . . . But what would the professor do about the letter "Y?""

"Oh, Louis," exclaimed Belle with delight and stopped writing.

"I am so very happy, Belle," said R. L. S.

CHAPTER II

THE IMP IN THE BOTTLE

TUSITALA, "The Teller of Tales," was the name given by the people of Samoa to Robert Louis Stevenson.

The Samoans loved Tusitala and saw in him the embodiment of happiness and wealth. Even before he built his fine new house, his native visitors had been amazed by his treasures; and his native servants spread his fame by telling fantastic stories about this man, who was quite different from other Papalangi; he was better, kinder, and also more glamorous, a greater chieftain. And now that the new palace was ready, all rumours, all legends and suppositions about Tusitala were confirmed.

Although the Samoans had never seen so beautiful a house before, they knew that such existed, for Tusitala himself had told them so. He had told them so the year before, and in a way which they were sure precluded any possible falsehood—namely in print.

The Christian missionaries had not only converted, but civilized and educated the brown folk of Samoa, and many could read everything that had been printed in Samoan. At that time this included the Bible, the Book of Common Prayer, the Hymnal and the Mission's magazine. Every word was sacred; every word was of course true.

The magazine, published by a London Missionary Society, was called in Samoan *O le Sulu o Samoa* and appeared weekly. It was very pious and undoubtedly a little dull until one day a wonderful story began to run in it, the first example of profane literature which had ever been printed in Samoan. It was called "The Bottle Imp" and the author—but what was an author?—was named Tusitala. There was no doubt that Tusitala was telling a true adventure.

Robert Louis Stevenson had followed a sudden impulse one day when he asked his good friend, Mr. Clarke, the missionary, if he might send over a fairy tale of the South Seas to be used in his pious publication. It was a Polynesian version of an old German legend; it had not yet been published in English when it was printed in the melodious dialect of the Samoans, and it ran through many exciting installments.

The hero of the story was a Kanaka named Keawe, or Teawe, as the Samoans pronounce it. The setting was in Hawaii, but that did not disturb the Samoan readers; they could easily see through such a slight subterfuge.

Keawe's house, which was carefully described in the beginning, could be identified by anyone who had eyes in his head.

There it was printed in black and white in the magazine.

30

"Now, the house stood on the mountain side, visible to ships. Above, the forest ran up into the clouds of rain; below, the black lava fell in cliffs, where the kings of old lay buried. A garden bloomed about that house with every hue of flowers; and there was an orchard of papaia on the one hand, and an orchard of herdprint on the other, and right in front, toward the sea, a ship's mast had been rigged up and bore a flag. As for the house, it was three stories high, with great chambers and broad balconies on each. The windows were of glass, so excellent that it was as clear as water and as bright as day. All manner of furniture adorned the chambers. Pictures hung upon the wall in golden frames—pictures of ships, and men fighting, and of the most beautiful women, and of singular places; nowhere in the world are there pictures of so bright a colour as those Keawe found hanging in his house. As for the knick-knacks, they were extraordinary fine: chiming clocks and musical boxes, little men with nodding heads, books filled with pictures, weapons of price from all quarters of the world, and the most elegant puzzles to entertain the leisure of a solitary man. And as no one would care to live in such chambers, only to walk through and view them, the balconies were made so broad that a whole town might have lived upon them in delight; and Keawe knew not which to prefer, whether the back porch, where you got the land breeze, and looked upon the orchards and the flowers, or the front balcony, where you could drink the wind of the sea. . . ."

Although the description did not tally in every detail, still the Samoan readers had no difficulty at all in recognizing Tusitala's new house in Vailima.

As the installments of "The Bottle Imp" appeared, the Samoans looked at each other more and more knowingly. They did not discuss the matter with the Papalangis, for the Samoans are an aristocratic people, full of reticence and fine sensibilities. When they talked among themselves, not one of them doubted that Tusitala and Keawe were one and the same person. They also saw in Keawe's wife Kokua (in the story) the mistress Aolele, Tusitala's consort.

Was not Tusitala like a fairy-tale hero and, like Keawe, fabulously rich? Was he not gay, like Keawe, of whom they had read in print that he could not go through his beautiful chambers without singing? And yet, when he thought himself unobserved, was he not overcome by a sudden sadness, a swift and mysterious foreshadowing of doom? Moreover, did it not also affect his wife? They called her Aolele, the Flying Cloud, because clouds crossed her face where an instant before she had smiled. She had smiled before Tusitala as a good wife should; but when the door had been closed on the room wherein Tusitala sat, the inhabitants of the house had often seen her face grow serious and dark. Did they not know of tears poured out in secret? It had all been mysterious, and now it became clear through Tusitala's tale of Keawe that he had bought all of his happiness and gold from the devil, in the shape of a certain magic vessel, in which a tiny little demon danced around like a shadow. You could give any command in the world to this little imp in the bottle, save only one. You could demand money and power, but not that your life be prolonged. That was obviously the reason why Tusitala was so often ill. The little imp could not cure him, but otherwise the possessor of the marvellous bottle could ask for anything, and the willing little demon would produce it in what was apparently the most natural possible way: a beautiful house, shiny dollars, tins of meat and salmon and countless other Papalangi delicacies, not to mention hogs, coconuts, taro root and kava.

Was the man happy who had bought the imp in the bottle? This is where the moral came in, for the sake of which the Christian missionary had translated the story into Samoan and published it in his pious magazine. How could anyone be happy who had entered into a pact with the devil!

Yet one could, according to the printed tale, rid oneself of the pact and of its symbol, the bottle. One had only to discover a man who would buy the terrible magic container, with all its riches and its curse, for a cheap price. The condition was that the price must be less than that paid by the present possessor. One other condition was that the price must be paid in coin, not in paper money or in goods. Whoever was lucky enough to find a rash buyer soon enough, so that he could rid himself of the bottle, escaped

33

(so ran Tusitala's really far from moral legend) the fearful consequences of his pact with the devil. Alas, however, for the last person who would die with the bottle still in his possession! Woe betide the foolish man who bought the diabolic treasure so cheaply that he could not be underbid by an even more foolish person! For in the end the Imp came out of the vessel, grew to terrible proportions and carried off the last owner.

The Samoans, although converted to Christianity, were not theologically very well informed, and they were not very familiar with the nature of the "Aitu" in the bottle. Samoa was full of native Aitus; they were hidden in every forest on the mountain, but they did not torment the souls of their victims for any metaphysic or moral reasons; they simply killed them in order to eat them afterwards. Samoa made no distinction between devil and death.

All Samoa said: Tusitala is good; he is powerful; even among the Papalangi no one is so rich as he. In the land of Queen Victoria he is a High Chief; he possesses fine mats. So Tusitala is happy, and one often sees him laugh; but when he is not observed, or thinks he is not, he is often sad; and the mistress Aolele often weeps when she is alone.

Either, concluded the Samoans among themselves, Tusitala cannot find a buyer for this marvellous but dangerous vessel, or, and this is quite possible, he was foolhardy enough to buy it for a cent; or worse, for one of those centimes which are current among the French Islands and which Kanaka sailors bring from Tahiti to Samoa. And now there is no price less than a copper centime piece. Even if he wished to, no one can buy the cursed thing now—that is why Tusitala, the happy one, is secretly sad; that is why Aolele weeps.

They have all the good fortune in the world; but they also have a bottle in the house, and in it, held only by a stopper, death awaits them.

CHAPTER III

THE PROCONSUL

ON the island of New Zealand in the Antipodes, February is a summer month. But the steamer *Mariposa* on which Louis, Fanny and Belle were taking a cruise to Australia after the flu epidemic, happened to be lying in the harbour of Auckland on a forbidding, rainy afternoon. Robert Louis Stevenson wanted to take advantage of being in this metropolis of New Zealand to make a call, so he left the ladies on board and went alone from the harbour into the town. He wore a raincoat and a white yachting cap, from whose patent-leather vizor the rain trickled. He had already sneezed once—and that with him was the first, as yet harmless, sign of a condition which might easily become dangerous. If Fanny had been along she would probably have insisted on his returning immediately to the ship and going to bed. But R. L. S. was alone and was, although he would not have admitted it, enjoying his little vacation from his womenfolk. He even enjoyed the cold rain which reminded him of Scotland, and the streets of the sprawling, ungainly colonial town of Auckland. It was neither a Paris nor an Edinburgh, but it had a much more European flavour than Apia. There were houses, gardens and trees that looked like the houses, gardens and trees back home. There were sidewalks, glistening in the rain, and there was a lady neatly holding up her long skirt. R. L. S., who had been wandering around in the South Seas now for five years, could imagine for a few seconds that he had escaped from his exile. Then he sneezed again and a sudden feeling of sadness came over him; it was like an invisible chain rattling on his leg. He had hardly arrived in a climate which, from a distance, made one think of Europe, when his inexorable destiny called out to him, "Back to your exile!"

However, there were many pleasant things to see along the way. There was even a first-class bookstore in Auckland; in the window, together with tracts on sheep raising, there were a few volumes of R. L. S.'s works: *Treasure Island, The Master of Ballantrae,* and his latest work, *The Wrecker,* had also reached the Antipodes and this particular showcase. R. L. S. was like other authors in that he could not withstand the temptation to go into the shop. He intended to buy something or other, and then incidentally inquire how Stevenson's new book was selling in New Zealand. But he could not carry out his design because the bookseller also handled illustrated papers and had recently seen a photograph of Stevenson, so he recognized his celebrated customer at once, and called him by name, which gave him a pleasant surprise. But then the famous man immediately adopted one of his poses and pretended he was not at all interested in

37

The Wrecker and asked for "something decent to read, nothing dull." The bookseller, who prided himself on getting all the latest things in modern literature direct from London, brought out volumes of Kipling and Barrie. But Stevenson saw *The Sins of the Countess* lying on the table and shockingly enough demanded some sensational novels of that sort. Having selected a pile of these penny dreadfuls, he ordered them sent aboard the *Mariposa*, adding, with a perfectly straight face, that he personally *always* read only trash. Then he asked to be directed to a certain hotel, the best in town, and went out, with a sly grin on his face. The bookseller was completely disillusioned. But he decided nevertheless to put a picture of Stevenson in the showcase with his books and added a little note to the effect: "On the occasion of the visit of this famous author to our city."

The famous author, still more or less incognito, went on through the rain-soaked streets of Auckland to the hotel, where he made inquiries and then sent his card up to a gentleman who was stopping there.

The head porter at the desk was a well-nourished, phlegmatic New Zealander, but when he saw the name on the visiting card and heard to whom it was being sent, he gave some slight signs of interest, and, speaking a little louder than was necessary, with a broad Cockney accent, he said: "Yes, indeed, Sir George is in." A bellboy, covered with gilt buttons, took charge of the thin stranger and led him, coughing slightly, up one flight of stairs. Meantime, the hotel dignitary at the desk buttonholed one of the guests who was passing by—to be exact it was a sheep farmer from Wanganui by the name of James T. Brown—and said, in a tone full of excitement for a New Zealander: "Look, Mr. Brown, that man over there is the chap who wrote *Treasure Island!*"

"Not possible!" commented Mr. Brown and looked around. For even out in the bush beyond Wanganui they were familiar with *Treasure Island.*

When the bellboy came in with the visiting card, an elderly gentleman, in a Prince Albert coat, rose from his armchair and came over to the door. He was over eighty and his trim beard, which protruded from between the two heavily starched wings of his choker, was quite white. His nose was long, straight, and thin as a blade; his forehead was powerful, and the blue eyes, under his humourous eyebrows, were unforgettable. This old gentleman was Sir George Grey, former Governor and Prime Minister of the Dominion of New Zealand. In the course of a long life dedicated to the service of the British Empire, he had also served as Governor of South Africa and South Australia. He had been a soldier, an explorer and a diplomat. He was one of the great statesmen Queen Victoria used as builders of the Empire. New Zealand owed him everything: its prosperity, its internal peace, its model social institutions, which had placed this exotic colony in the front rank of the progressive countries of that day. Nevertheless, Sir George had tasted of the proverbial ingratitude of democracies and had been through many bitter experiences. Now he was living in retirement on an island not far from Auckland, and he used this hotel room only when he had business in town.

There they stood: the Great Proconsul of the South Seas and the Great Poet of the South Seas. And from the first second of their encounter, there sprang up a feeling of sympathy between them, as between father and son. They were two contrasting types of Anglo-Saxon manhood; the elder man was heavy, massive, imposing, and the younger one was delicate, jumpy, full of restlessness and movement. Yet one look, one gesture, sufficed to make the contact. Sir George laid his great hand on Stevenson's thin shoulders for a moment, and won his friendship for life.

They were Britons, so naturally they did not fall on each other's necks, nor did they even start the conversation with any effusive remarks; they spoke to each other as Great Powers do, in a tone of grave courtesy, which was second nature to the statesman and which even a bohemian like Stevenson could very well assume when needed. Just as visiting potentates wear each other's uniforms on formal occasions, Stevenson used subtle flattery on the Grand Old Man of the South Seas, not by alluding to his political prominence which was his real life work, but to his literary achievements, which were a by-product. Sir George had written an excellent work on Polynesian mythology and had collected both sayings and songs. Stevenson spoke of this with great respect.

Grey, on the other hand, saluted the uniform of his own regiment, put on for the occasion by his distinguished guest, by not referring to *Treasure Island* or the other novels, essays or poems which had made Stevenson famous. No, he spoke to him in terms of praise for his achievements as a colonial statesman, as the friend and champion of the brown people of Samoa.

Stevenson had called on Sir George for the purpose of discussing with him the political situation in the Samoa Archipelago. This Island kingdom, of which R. L. S. was now an inhabitant, was suffering from a severe crisis. In giving up its old barbaric ways and turning to Christianity, Samoa had come in contact with the civilization of the whites and lost its former independence. Not that it had been annexed by any of the Great Powers; the crisis arose from the fact that three of them, Germany, Great Britain and the United States, were fighting among themselves over it. To be sure, they had found, a few years previously, a temporary diplomatic solution to the ridiculous but nevertheless dangerous Samoan Question.

Since they could not agree for the time being on the partitioning of Samoa, and yet were not inclined to let the Samoans govern their own country, they had erected a

Co-Dominion. That is to say that, under the Berlin-Samoan Convention, the Samoans were to elect their own king "according to Samoan custom"—of which the diplomats did not have even a vague notion—and he was to be recognized by the three Great Powers. Actually, however, the consuls of these same powers, together with their white "Advisers," were to run the government for which the Samoans would pay. Also there was to be a "President of the Municipality of Apia" and a "Chief Justice." An International Territorial Commission was to see that foreign planters obtained the best land for their coconut plantations. "Order" was to be guaranteed by the guns of foreign battleships. Otherwise, the Polynesian population of Samoa was completely free and independent and had every right, as far as a half-dozen different varieties of missionaries permitted, to go to the devil "according to Samoan custom."

In this way everything had been beautifully arranged and, except for the Samoans, who really did not count, no one in the whole wide world had raised the slightest objection; no one except Tusitala, a delicate invalid storyteller from Scotland, who accidentally—but are such things really accidents?—had come to Samoa shortly after the signing of the wonderful Berlin Convention, to cheat death of a few more years from his life.

There the two men sat, Sir George on the sofa and opposite him Robert Louis Stevenson, in the armchair reserved for guests. It was very difficult for him to sit there quietly, and it was quite impossible for him to refrain from smoking his English cigarettes, although it would have been more proper for him not to smoke. He himself felt that he was participating in a kind of audience of state with one of the great men of the earth and that he ought to make a serious impression. But for all that, he had not been able to bring himself even to put on a stiff collar or any more formal clothes than his usual velvet jacket. So here they sat, the statesman and the Bohemian artist, talking across a table laden with books and newspapers. It was not without emotion that Stevenson caught sight, among the pamphlets lying there, of a little brochure he himself had written about the Samoan situation and entitled *A Foot-note to History*. Also on the table were copies of the *Times* with Stevenson's letters from Samoa. In short, Sir George was not only extremely well posted on the happenings in Samoa, but was also aware of Stevenson's share in them.

"What is your friend Mataafa doing?" asked the elder statesman, and a fleeting, humourous twinkle in his remarkable blue eyes indicated that the old gentleman had not inquired by chance after the Samoan chieftain Mataafa. The fact that this popular but unsuccessful pretender to the Samoan throne enjoyed the preference and protection of Tusitala was well known at this time on every white beach of the South Seas, in every water-front saloon, in every shop, in every pearl fisher's boat; and it was known in the

Foreign Office in London. People who had no interest at all in Samoa cracked sorry jokes over R. L. S. and his pet nigger, Mataafa, so stubbornly and so cleverly had Stevenson presented his case to British public opinion through the columns of the *Times*—his case for Mataafa, who, it seemed to him, was better fitted to rule Samoa than his cousin and rival, Laupepa. Stevenson readers throughout the world had discovered through his curious *Foot-note to History* how and to what extent this old white-moustached Kanaka, who said his beads religiously, had a proper right to the Samoan throne. (In the eyes of the Samoans it was a question, not of the throne, but of certain titles and of antique, finely woven mats which were the real basis for any claim to be a High Chief.) In this pamphlet Stevenson had treated the tragicomic cat-and-dog fight in Samoa with all the seriousness a writer of the Renaissance would have given to the struggles between Guelphs and Ghibellines in Pisa or Florence. In his conversation with the old Victorian statesman, R. L. S. might think he was playing the part of a Machiavelli of the South Seas; but instead of that, if the truth were told, he felt suddenly that he was in a rather ridiculous position. In this room the importance of Samoa somehow seemed to shrink. Who, indeed, was Mataafa? Was it really of so great moment whether he bore the feudal title of "Malietoa" rightfully or whether Laupepa usurped it? It was not a question of whether one or another of the Samoan chieftains succeeded in seizing a phantom kingdom for himself. The

44

point was whether all the brown peoples of the Polynesian Islands should have the right to their own lives and could assert themselves in their own way against the white intruders.

As the two men sat there, it was easy to distinguish between the two racial strains that go to make up Great Britain —the Saxon and the Celt. Sir George had blue eyes, was reserved and powerful; Stevenson was darker, more graceful, full of temperament. It was as though Puck were calling on Wotan, to give him a report. Stevenson had begun by speaking in a rather embarrassed, shy way; then he had been carried away by the momentum of his own flow of words, his self-hypnotic power of expression which brushed aside his inner lack of assurance. He drew a highly idealized picture of Mataafa and painted it with all the richly romantic colour of a storyteller; under his loving brush Mataafa emerged as a Samoan "Bonny Prince Charlie," whose adventures in 1745 are graven on the heart of every Scotsman, and whom Stevenson himself had glorified in his books. The Samoan Pretender was sitting at this very moment, threatening and stubborn, in his tent or his beehive-shaped hut in the village of Malie, ready to rise against his cousin, King Laupepa, who to him was a mere usurper.

R. L. S. talked on, and Sir George, the experienced political veteran, listened attentively without interrupting. His eyes were fixed on an old copy of the *Times* and his hand, with a seal ring on one of his fingers, played lightly with a massive paper cutter. Perhaps as he sat there and listened to Stevenson's impassioned plea for the liberty of the Polynesians in Samoa, Sir George was thinking that a generation earlier he himself had been largely responsible for the robbing of the cousins of the Samoans, the New Zealand Maoris, of their land, and forcibly subjecting them to the civilization of the whites. Such a well-informed diplomat could hardly be unaware that the fate of the Samoans, as well as that of all the other South Sea Islanders, was already sealed. England and France, as possessors of the most beautiful and fertile island in the Pacific, had already sated their appetites; Hawaii was in the last stages of a hopeless struggle to escape the toils of the Americans; in Samoa the real point at issue was not whether a Mataafa or a Laupepa should pretend to rule, but whether the Archipelago would be divided between America and Germany, and under what conditions; and what price England would exact for withdrawing her claims. It was a struggle to see who would get the harbour of Pago-Pago, which was destined to become an important naval base, and who would control the economically and strategically less important remainder of the Archipelago; that was the real basis of the contest and not the internal quarrels of chieftains.

All this was clear enough to the elderly empire-builder of the South Seas, as he listened while Stevenson talked on with the tongue of an angel. Yet at the same time he was that

46

same George Grey who had been so carried away by the beautiful Polynesian myths. He seemed to see Maui, god and hero, fishing the islands out of the water; his mind's eye followed the viking-like expedition of the Polynesians, who started from some mythical homeland in their long beautifully carved canoes, and went from archipelago to archipelago, as conquerors and colonizers. He knew that the same vowel-laden language was spoken in Hawaii, New Zealand, Tahiti, Tonga, Samoa, the Marquesas Islands and elsewhere in that wide-flung Empire of Islands. He knew, too, that these flower-bedecked peoples, who spoke this loveliest of all languages, were probably the most charming, hopeful and promising young nation which had arisen on this earth since the downfall of Greece. They were barbarians, yes, and not so very long ago they had been cannibals —but was not Minos of Crete a barbarian? Did the Minotaur not eat men? Yet was not Cretan culture the fountainhead of Hellenic civilization? The Polynesians were that last untapped source of youth in the world, with all the gay virgin quality, naïve enjoyment of beauty, intelligently happy innocence, that goes with being young in heart. But that was before Captain Cook's fateful journey of discovery a century ago, and now all this was a thing of the past. No one realized it more keenly than the wise old English Colonial Governor as he listened to a poet's excited tale. But that was all a dream; the Polynesians must make way, as the Maoris had done in New Zealand, where their land had been used for the largest and most successful experiment in colonization which the nineteenth century had seen. In Hawaii the soil was needed for sugar cane, and in other parts of the South Seas copra was king. All this was clear and had to be; nevertheless, it was a joy to hear this emaciated man with shining eyes talk about the tragedy of the Polynesians, the Greeks of the South Seas, who were doomed to go under before they had brought forth their Homer, their Phidias or their Plato!

When Stevenson, who had talked too long, had a fit of coughing and was obliged to stop, Sir George rose and stood over him for some time, with a faint, knowing smile on his face. Then he began to nod his head, like a wise old porcelain mandarin, and said: "Thank God, you are not so ill as I feared." Then he looked at Stevenson pleadingly, and his coughing stopped at once. Sir George nodded his old head again and said:

"You may think I am old-fashioned, but I believe in destiny. You think it was chance that brought you to the South Seas. But there is a power above us. When I heard that you, a man with romantic imaginative capacities, had settled out here, I said to myself—it has happened, and now this noble people of the South Seas cannot vanish entirely."

He insisted on escorting Robert Louis Stevenson downstairs and through the lobby of the hotel. The other guests saw the Grand Old Man of the South Seas stiffly but tenderly put his arm around the thin shoulders of the writer. The bootblack at the door of the hotel was watching for R. L. S. in order to tell him, with a New Zealand Cockney accent, that he had read all of his stories. Then an almost incredible thing happened: Stevenson paid no attention to the compliment. He did not even know that the bootblack had spoken to him, or that the guests in the hotel had stared at him as though he were some strange animal. He walked through the streets of Auckland, right through all the puddles, like one possessed, his head deep between his shoulders. Sir George Grey himself had told him that what he was doing in Samoa was not nonsense and a waste of time. "Destiny has sent you to Samoa, my dear Mr. Stevenson!"

No shadow of doubt lay on his feeling of happiness. It did not even occur to him that the great statesmen was perhaps not thinking of the chieftain's quarrel and of his propaganda on behalf of Mataafa, when he was speaking of destiny and the role of a poet in the South Seas. Robert Louis Stevenson did not even think, at that moment, of his poems, his several novels, his travel diary, in which he had captured for all time the enchantment of the South Seas.

The intoxication and exaltation of his happy mood wore gradually away in the cool damp air, but his good humour remained. He thought tenderly now of Fanny and Belle, who had stayed on the ship and not participated in his triumph. He wanted to take them some lovely present; something with jewels in it.

He stood for a while in front of a jeweler's shop, but could not find anything suitable in the window. After all, it would be better to have some rings made in Sydney. With topazes. Topaz is the lucky stone for people born in November; his birthstone. So there would be topaz rings for Fanny and Belle; they would look so well on their sun-tanned fingers. He even decided to treat himself to a topaz ring. And Lloyd— R. L. S. hesitated for a moment over whether he should order a fourth ring for Lloyd Osbourne, and then decided to give him something much more expensive. A pair of cuff links set with sapphires. There would be only the three rings. And the verses with which he would present them began to take shape in his mind:

> "These rings, o my beloved pair,
> For me on your brown fingers wear . . ."

He went on to develop his idea: When you wake up in the morning and feel these rings caress your fingers, think of him who is awake before you, who has a ring too on his finger, which he kisses, earnestly and solemnly, breathing a blessing on you, my dears. . . ."

At first these rhymes did not come to him with the effortless lightness he required; but as he stood there in the rain, in front of the jewellery store, where he had had two more coughing fits, he decided that on the next day, when they would be on their way to Sydney, he would walk up and down the deck and finish the verses.

CHAPTER IV

AITU FAFINE

THE name of the plantation, Vailima, in Samoan means Five Rivers. When the Stevensons bought the three hundred acres of virgin bush along the foot of Mount Vaea, and were choosing a name for this property, full of babbling woodland streams, R. L. S. had liked the soft-sounding syllables of Vai and Lima, meaning River and Five; and now that the house was built, and the young cocoa trees were planted and growing, the owner of Vailima liked frequently to roam about his land and count the rivers. There was a quantity of both foaming and majestically smooth-flowing waters in Vailima; they fell in flashing cascades from the high rocks, or lay in broad pools, where coconut palm and orange trees were reflected, and naked brown folk bathed at all hours. Light bridges spanned the streams; canoes travelled up and down them. Every path in Vailima led to lovely, warm, tropical waters, filled with fish and delectable little crawfish. But why five rivers? If one counted every little rivulet, there were more than five. If one judged the matter in terms of real rivers then, by the most liberal reckoning and with the best will in the world, one could not find more than three streams of generous proportions in addition to the Vaea River. Either the fifth river of Vailima flowed through the secret places of unexplored bush, or it flowed not at all. This worried the writer who had given his estate a name flowing with vowels and rivers; so without telling anyone, or even admitting the reason to himself, he often went into the forest behind the house to search for the fifth river.

His household thought he was taking a walk to gather ideas for a chapter in some novel. Or they thought, and here they smiled privately to themselves, that he was going off to play on his flageolet. For he had a great affection, which was, alas, not requited, for this shrill little instrument, and he drove his hearers to distraction when he played on it; so he often took it out into the woods with him. But when the distant notes had died away, and Fanny and Lloyd thought he was practicing in some thicket in the bush, actually he was breaking all his physicians' orders, climbing around, breathing heavily and perspiring freely, in the forest on the mountain slope, hoping to discover the fifth stream—and perhaps, too, Aitu Fafine, the beautiful and dangerous water sprite who, according to legends, lived in it.

Stevenson had undertaken just such a trip of exploration one day, a few weeks after his return to Samoa. The journey, made for the sake of his health, to Auckland and Sydney, had failed of its purpose. On the trip Louis had caught a heavy cold and was quite ill aboard ship. Back home Fanny fell a victim to the grippe; now she was better, but had given the germ to Lloyd, who was at the moment laid up.

For Stevenson to catch a cold was a serious catastrophe; consequently, when any member of his household was affected, he was obliged to isolate himself to avoid contagion. Lloyd Osbourne lived alone in a tiny cottage on the grounds, but as his mother naturally came over often to see him while he was ill, she kept away from Louis as much as possible for fear of transmitting germs to her husband. She was working with her characteristic energy in the garden that day when he went through it in the cool of the afternoon; so she waved a spade at him from a distance. She was dressed in a native Holoku skirt, a sort of longish apron which was covered from top to bottom with dirt. Fanny Stevenson (born Van de Grift) had inherited from her Dutch ancestors a passion for gardening; she had full scope now to try out a thousand experiments in the garden at Vailima. Sometimes Louis worked with her, setting out cocoa trees with his own hands until his back ached. But today he was under the restrictions of the taboo, and when he made a move to come near his wife, he was energetically shooed away. He stood around for a while listening to the incredible mixture of American English and mispronounced Samoan in which his wife was talking to Simele, who was helping her with the work.

Then R. L. S. moved off until the sounds of Fanny's energetic voice and Simele's quiet and dignified answers, in the tone suitable to a High Chief, were no longer audible.

The garden proper was soon left behind; a light bridge took him over a stream, whose left bank he followed until he came to a marsh, where there was a plantation of broad-leaved giant bananas. There he found a huge Samoan by the name of Lafaele, dressed only in a short skirt and working among the banana foliage; sweat was pouring off his carefully oiled torso. His greeting was: "Talofa, Tusitala! My love is yours, Tusitala." "Talofa," answered Tusitala gravely. The young Samoan seemed about to say something to deter him from going on; then he swallowed whatever words were on his lips and remained silent. Stevenson smiled; he knew that whenever this overgrown chocolate-colored child, this young Hercules with the name of an archangel, was sent into the banana plantation on the edge of the jungle, he was simply terrified. But Fanny persisted in sending him there. This spot was comparatively near the main house, and therefore not too fearsome; yet even here Lafaele had at least once distinctly heard the whistling of the devil, who lived just a little farther on, beyond the clumps of bananas. If anyone went on beyond the bananas into the darkest bush, he would most certainly come to a region where he must be prepared to meet with some horror. Lafaele was unable to comprehend how anybody would willingly go alone into the woods which everyone in Samoa knew were inhabited by a woman fiend. Lafaele had passionately warned Tusitala against this siren more than once, and he felt impelled to warn him again now; but he did not do it, because each time he had been laughed at. After all, the Samoans realized that the Papalangi, and especially a High Chief like Tusitala, had their own magic with which to counteract the charms of the native spirits; presumably this Kanaka dryad would be helpless before the man who had his own private imp stopped up in a bottle! So Lafaele was satisfied to give a serious and significant greeting to Tusitala, and let him go on, beyond the banana plantation, up the stream into the wilderness.

The Samoan children did not seem to be so fearful of the witch of the bushland as Lafaele, for a good deal farther on R. L. S. met two children, stark naked, except for some garlands of gay colored seeds around their necks; it was a little boy with large eyes, with his tiny sister. They had evidently been bathing in some upstream pool—without giving a though to the Aitu!—and they had caught some crawfish which the boy had wrapped in a taro leaf and was triumphantly taking home. And although they were undoubtedly little poachers on Tusitala's property, the children were completely unabashed and entirely cordial in their greeting: "Talofa, Alii"—our love is yours, great chieftain—and they ran off laughing. The little girl had stuck a scarlet hibiscus flower behind her tiny ear. "My love to you, children," said Robert Louis Stevenson, and at that moment he felt literally the words of the lovely native greeting; for no one could help loving all Samoan children, quite regardless of what these little laughing, elfin creatures might grow up to be.

Perhaps I can include these two naked tots in my next letter to Adelaide, thought R. L. S. Adelaide was a Miss Boodle, a young lady with literary inclinations whom Stevenson had known in Bournemouth. At present she was teaching kindergarten for children of English working people, and Stevenson sometimes sent her letters which were really intended for her pupils. He had the idea, in the back of his mind, that these letters might later on be collected into a children's book of the South Seas. So he always wrote to Adelaide about subjects of interest to children and in a juvenile style. In these letters he figured as the "Lean Man," and he liked to think of himself as the Lean Man of his children's letters as he rambled around in this fairy-tale forest in the tropics. Naturally, as the famous Robert Louis Stevenson, the blasé fin-de-siècle writer, the frequenter of Paris cafés and rendezvous of artists in Montparnasse and Barbizon, the member of London's Savile Club, he could never for an instant admit that the mysterious call of a bird out of the depths of the dark Samoan forest, or the inexplicable sound of some invisible axe, could deeply frighten him. But as the Lean Man, he could confess to all such childish terrors, and he could state quite frankly that he was afraid of a Samoan wood witch, who roamed the forest around Vailima in the form of a gorgeous golden-skinned woman with red hair, looking for men to destroy. They said: a man wandering in the forest suddenly feels a current of air, and there she stands smiling before him in all her radiant beauty. But to meet her, the witch Aitu Fafine, means death! Yes, he was afraid, but like some naughty boy he was thrilled by it. He was drawn irresistibly on and on into the mysterious forest, reeking with tropical decay, wild oranges and orchids.

This Lean Man, who was also a sick man, who should probably not have attempted to climb the mountain on so sultry an afternoon, was dressed in a pair of loose linen slacks, a shirt wide open at the neck, and his bare feet were stuck into sandals. His shirt was wet with perspiration and clung to his body. The heat in the forest was damp. There was no refreshing breeze from the sea today; everything was dank and still or else filled with mysterious noises. The Lean Man, or rather the grown-up who was identified with this storybook figure, knew perfectly well that woods in this bush region of Samoa were quite empty and safe, that there were almost no mammals and no snakes. There was really nothing in this particular jungle to give any sensible person cause for alarm. At the most, there might be a few wild hogs at large, which it would be wise to avoid. There were unfounded rumours going around about cannibals. These were black boys, natives of islands in Melanesia, whom the German planters had imported to work on their cocoa plantations. Occasionally they ran away into the bush, either because of the harshness of the conditions of work or cruelty on the part of overseers, and they were supposed to have reverted to cannibalism. Nothing was known for certain, although there was a great deal of talk on the subject. Stevenson was not afraid of them; but what was that sound? It was like a dog's bark, yet it must be a bird because it came from the branches overhead. Then there was another bird—was it really a bird?—which began to cry like a child. At that instant the wailing cry pierced to the very marrow of one's bones! To drown out the sound—surely not because the Lean Man was filled with a nameless fear—R. L. S. drew his flute out of his pocket; it just occurred to him that he had wanted to practice in the woods. So when he reached a small clearing he stopped, wiped away the perspiration that was streaming down his forehead from under his long hair, put his silver-mounted flute to his lips and blew harder than the bird could wail.

There he stood, a complex human being with many facets to his personality: he was Tusitala, a High Chief in Samoa, and he was the children's Lean Man, afraid of a bird's cry. He was also the famous author Robert Louis Stevenson, who was secretly observing that Lean Man because he was intending to write a series of letters from Polynesia for children. And he was a soul hungering for music, who did not dare practice on his flute in his own house, as well as a sick man, a prisoner in the climate of the South Seas; in sum, he was R. L. S. At first he found it hard to pipe, for his poor lungs were tired and out of breath. This made him think of Lloyd Osbourne, who had still not built a passable road to the top of Mt. Vaea, where R. L. S. would one day be buried. He wanted it to be that way, and he believed in his own death as much as anyone believes in it—which is to say, not at all.

58

Then he piped another shrill passage. He had always longed to play some instrument and never had an opportunity to satisfy his feeling until now. It was characteristic of him that, having weak lungs, he would set himself to master a wind instrument; a piano or a violin would have given him far less enjoyment. His family was little interested in music, and they were horrified by his flute, so he never could really learn to play on it. Lloyd Osbourne's irony on the subject, although good-natured, was still irony, and it was a sore spot with Stevenson. So he stood here in the wilderness and blew on his flute; and did it badly. From where he stood he could look far down, through the trees of the tropical forest, to the heavy, dark blue surface of the sea and the glaring white band of breakers outlining the island of Upolu. Now his notes on the flute turned into a cry, a plaintive sighing; it was all so unreal, so improbable, this whole mad adventure; these South Seas, this ado about the Antipodes, where he was stranded. Was this really he, R. L. S., who had been imprisoned for five full years in this vast expanse of islands, lagoons and atolls? For he was a prisoner. Although he could travel by steamer, schooner or bark from one corner of this endless gaol to another out on the rim of the earth, he could not escape entirely. Here he must remain to the bitter end, always and forever gazing at the glaring water, the eternally blue sky, the pitiless sunlight!

59

The wretchedly ill man flung his flute to the ground in a sudden outburst of anguished rage.

Five years out of a total of only forty-two! And who knew for how many more, no, for how few more it was to last! (A glance at Mt. Vaea; yes, it was there, always oppressively present.) All at once it seemed to Robert Louis Stevenson that the first thirty-seven years of his life had been a time of pure happiness; he forgot that as an ailing invalid he had spent the greater part of that time leading a miserable existence in all sorts of health resorts on the Riviera, in Davos, Hyères, Bournemouth, and that it was really here in the South Seas that he had been able to enjoy freely a normal life for months and years. What kind of life? Somewhere in Europe, in a concert hall, at this very time, Pablo Sarasate was playing on his violin, Paderewski on his piano; and when R. L. S. wanted some music he could go out into the wilderness and squeak a tune to himself on this cursed flageolet (here he ground it under his heel), or else he could go into a saloon along the Apia water front and get a drunken sailor to play an accordion for him!

Before a newspaper could reach Apia, it was a month old; if you were writing an historical novel and needed to check a reference, a name, a date, a detail of any kind, you could send a letter to London and very likely wait six months for the desired information. Everything was so frightfully far away, libraries, publishers, newspapers, magazines, friends. . . .

60

Then R. L. S. suddenly realized that what he really missed in Samoa was his friends. The new life which he had built up out here in the South Seas for himself, for Fanny and her children, was very different from that of his youth, but it was beautiful and worth while. If only he could show it to the people he loved back home, to the friends of his childhood; if only they could have joined in his new game—"Tusitala."

A sharp, swift pang went through Robert Louis Stevenson's soul as he remembered fleetingly the dearest of the friends of his youth, whom he had lost, not through death, but, as many men lose their friends, through marriage. William Ernest Henley, the poet, was, like Stevenson, an invalid, and perhaps for that reason he had held him particularly dear. But he could not get on with Fanny and had become, alas, if not an enemy, at least a stranger to him. There was nothing he could do about that; but in the cities of Europe and America were other friends, travelling companions and comrades, writers, painters, some successful, some still bohemians: Henry James, Sidney Colvin, Charles Baxter, Will Low. There they all were in their great cool cities, living their lives in familiar surroundings, and occasionally, for a moment, one of them would think of his friend Stevenson, poor fellow, and would write him a letter with a bit of gayety in it or a touch of rough comradely humour. And there were other men in that world of theirs—whom he knew only slightly or not at all—men he would have enjoyed—Rodin, Rudyard Kipling, J. M. Barrie, Conan Doyle—men whom he knew only by correspondence. The year before, Kipling had announced that he was coming to Samoa; R. L. S. was down at the harbour to meet him. The ship came in, but no Kipling was on board. Charles Baxter and Sidney Colvin both had promised to come out; perhaps not all the way to Samoa, for they were now men with responsibilities and offices and their leaves of absence were not unlimited. But one might go as far as Honolulu to meet them, or even a bit farther. Perhaps—and at the very thought of this joyous possibility the exile caught his breath—perhaps he could spend a winter in Madeira; the climate there was supposed to be similar to that of the South Seas. And Madeira is only a few days out of Liverpool; one could see one's friends there, and perhaps, in the hot days of midsummer, one might venture to go over for a few days to Scotland. . . .

Oh, the fragrance of the heather in bloom on the slopes of Ben Lomond, the clouds wreathed around the lonely mountain-tops in the Highlands, the chaste, cool Scottish sun playing on the waves of Loch Katrine, the grey streets of Edinburgh and the beloved Castle Rock clustered about with so many memories!

The Samoan forest was quite deserted. Not a living soul saw Robert Louis Stevenson weep.

Was there really no one there to see him? He suddenly felt that he was not alone in the clearing. Perhaps the impassable green wall of the jungle thicket did not open before his frenzied eyes, did not dissolve, but instead changed to clear green glass; and through it he saw, indistinctly at first, and then more and more clearly, a fresh stream of water that had not been there before. He knew at once that it was the long-sought-for fifth river. Wild orange trees grew along its banks; a naked woman with a beautiful bosom sat smiling in a boat, letting the water run over her bare legs. She had the golden brown skin and features of a Kanaka girl, but her hair was not black; it had a marvellous sheen of reddish gold, an effect the Samoan women try to get by dyeing their locks with a compound of powdered shells. But the red of her hair was unearthly, and woven into it was a garland of heavily scented jasmine blossoms. She had no vestige of clothing on her gorgeous body. Robert Louis Stevenson knew the Samoan legends and immediately recognized the very nymph, the female demon, about whom the Lean Man had sent to the children in Miss Boodle's school a half-fearsome, half-ironical letter. Yes, this was Aitu Fafine, the phantom witch of Samoa, who appears in the form of a marvellously beautiful woman to lonely men and smiles at them; but to see her and desire her means death. He even knew her real name, Saumai Afe, which means: "Come here a thousand!" She had already smiled on thousands of men, and stretched out to them her necklace of scarlet berries, a death-dealing gift.

She smiled and slowly loosed her scarlet necklace from

around her throat. Then Stevenson, another Odysseus, suddenly knew her. She had already lured thousands to that death, swallowed them up, this smiling, radiant siren—the South Seas.

Then for an instant the dreamer thought he saw some resemblance to Fanny's features in the face of the phantom. Had she lured him away from all of his friends, from his own life, from the pulsing life of Europe to this deathtrap, on the banks of the Fifth River of Vailima, to this enchanting but deadly paradise of sirens in the blue ocean? The sudden thought vanished as abruptly as it had come, and with it the resemblance between Aitu Fafine and Fanny or any other woman; even the apparition itself seemed to pale.

Into the sultry, breathless, motionless jungle there suddenly swept such a violent gust of wind that the branches on the trees lashed about like serpents gone mad. Dead leaves and nuts flew through the air; for a moment one could not see anything, and then the impassable green wall of the jungle closed in. The vision had disappeared into the steaming air, and with it the Fifth River. The Lean Man, the invalid poet, stood all alone in the clearing, on the slope of Mt. Vaea, and in spite of the heavy heat of the afternoon he felt a chill go through him. Down below, a breeze ruffled the surface of the sea. As Robert Louis Stevenson, quite bewildered, leaned over to pick up his flageolet, a large green lizard with a sapphire blue tail scurried away, startled by his sudden movement. Stevenson stuck his flute into his trousers pocket and made his way down the mountain side, first forcing himself to walk slowly, then going faster and faster until he was stumbling, breathlessly, over stick and stone. Finally he lost all sense of shame and put down his head and ran. In the forest there was a smell of death and decay, and a strange bird was calling from some bush. It sounded like the wail of a child.

CHAPTER V

ON THE BEACH

THE word beach has a special connotation in the countries of the South Seas; it is the home of the beachcombers, sailors who have deserted from their ships, ruined traders, ex-missionaries or aristocrats. From among them are recruited the deadhead drunkards of the water-front saloons, the sponging clientele of the opium dens and the illegitimate husbands of dusky princesses.

When Robert Louis Stevenson was living in Samoa, a very young beachcomber was cutting a great swathe on the beach at Apia, and in the hinterland on the island of Upolu. He was barely twenty, an Englishman of good parentage; he had run away to sea when he was fourteen. Everyone called this vagabond "Middy," not because he had seen service on a battleship and reached the rank of midshipman, but because it sounded a little like his own name. Middy had a talent for music and fiddled creditably; his art had helped him on his way through the world. He had been on many an adventurous journey, shipping as cabin boy, sailor, steward, or in some similar capacity, but he had also spent nights on the park benches of Sydney in company with vagabonds and criminals. Many a dusky island king, and cannibal chieftain too, potentates of the widely scattered insular domains of the South Seas, had had him give command performances on his "spirit wood," as they liked to call his violin, and in return had laden him with coconuts and breadfruit. If at this particular time he was hanging around Samoa, instead of going to sea or into the Australian gold mines, it was for the sake of the bright eyes and golden complexion of a Samoan maiden. Her name was Papoo, and she lived in her father's hut on the slopes of Mt. Vaea, not very far from Stevenson's house. Her father was a Matai of chieftain rank, but not a true High Chief who would be allowed to sit in the Fono, the council of chieftains, with his back against one of the pillars which support the round structure of the meeting-house, as those of higher rank may do. The idea that his daughter was having an affair with a Papalangi who lived "on the beach" did not please this respectable, tattooed, Samoan paterfamilias, and he was far from thinking that it was an honour. That is why Middy could come to Papoo, and bring his violin, only when her father was absent. On such occasions Middy would steal through the bush to her hut, and she would run out to meet him. She would be dressed in a short, fiery-red skirt, fashioned out of a flannel nightshirt which had belonged to an old sea captain; otherwise her young body was comparatively uncovered, although to be sure it was rubbed with coconut oil until it glistened, and she was further adorned with a number of wreaths of flowers and necklaces.

Yet it must be said that Middy, in his worn and frayed sailor clothes, was no fashion plate either. Unmindful of all this, the two young people were very much in love and, in spite of Papoo's papa, very happy. While Middy played strange melodies of the Papalangi on his fiddle, Papoo listened with wide eyes. Then she in turn sang Polynesian songs to him, and accompanied them with dance steps; to his musical ear the Samoan songs were soft and lovely. After the concert Papoo fed her troubadour with Kanaka delicacies. This was a charming little South Seas idyll, and perhaps the youngsters might have carried out their plan and run away to Australia, might have struck gold, might have lived happy forever after—if Papoo's father had not discovered their tricks and if there had not been a terrible and memorable row, which brought the little romance to a catastrophic end. But all this does not belong to the story of Tusitala.

One day, after Papoo's father had begun to have serious suspicions of their goings on and therefore they had to be careful to keep out of his sight, the lovers had arranged to meet in a lonely spot not far from the beach. Middy and Papoo sat on a stump under a coco palm and talked together in a weird mixture of English and Polynesian, for they could not make themselves understood in any one language; they sighed a little and poured out the contents of their broken young hearts. Not that Middy's heart was so irretrievably broken that he did not have the strength, from time to time, to play his violin. Once, too, he took time out to climb a near-by tree and bring down from its crest a delicately woven bird's nest, filled with tiny speckled eggs. Middy and Papoo were examining the eggs when they became aware of a thin man who was lying in the dense shade not far from them, and who had either not noticed the pair of lovers or was not concerned with them. There he sat on the ground, or rather reclined, against a tree trunk, whence he could look through the coco palms out to the shimmering sea. He was simply clad, in white, and he had drawn his knees up so that his long bony legs could serve as a writing desk for him; he had a pad with him, and, from time to time, he wrote down a few lines.

"That is Tusitala," said the Samoan girl softly; and suddenly she vanished among the tree trunks as a lizard slips away. Evidently she had not wanted to be seen by the stranger. Her friend Middy did not know what was meant by the word "Tusitala." So he continued to sit there out of idle curiosity. As a matter of fact, he was not disinclined to enter into conversation with the unknown man, who might be a planter or a copra trader, and therefore a useful acquaintance for a beachcomber. So he fiddled away until the stranger finally became aware of the noise and came over to him. He saw the bird's nest lying on the ground and the eggs in it, and the first thing he wanted to know was what kind of a bird had laid those eggs. Middy had no idea; sailors are not very well posted on birds' nests. The gentleman then showed an interest in Middy's violin, and asked if he might try to play on it. That he was a gentleman Middy had been able to deduce with the unerring instinct of a Britisher. But he could not play the violin for all his tapering and delicately formed hands, so necessary to a performer on that instrument. Otherwise he did not seem at all awkward, and he gave proof of some musical ear; but he soon gave up the attempt, with a little sigh, bade Middy good day in a friendly fashion and went off about his own affairs; obviously he was looking for solitude and not for conversation. As soon as he had gone, Papoo reappeared and said that that was Tusitala, Tusitala himself. But Middy had not taught her enough Beach-English to enable her to explain to her lover just who and what Tusitala was.

A few days later Middy was walking along the beach of Apia with his bosom friend Horncastle. Horncastle was an elderly seaman who, mysteriously enough, had money to spend on drinks and often spent it in Middy's company, so that the latter had reason to think well of him. But Middy liked him, too, for the numberless tales of true or imaginary adventures which Horncastle knew how to tell. The two of them were lounging along the beach slowly when that same white gentleman whom Middy had seen recently, and whom his girl had called "Tusitala," rode by on a brown horse in the direction of the German Hotel. Old Horncastle told him it was the famous writer, Robert Louis Stevenson—a bit queer, you know, my boy, but a fine fellow, one of the best; he added that he was on terms of great intimacy with him. Now Middy, the young beachcomber, who in his leisure time pretended to do a little writing, had never read a line of Stevenson, although he was very familiar with his reputation. It rather tickled his vanity that he had spoken alone, and familiarly too, with this renowned writer, and he was anxious to hear more about him. So he was extremely enthusiastic in the acceptance of his red-nosed buddy's invitation to go to the shell shop and have a drink.

The shell shop was a wooden shanty out at the far end of the beach, and it belonged to a half-breed. The man really did do business in shells and coral, but he also served drinks. The furnishings of the inside of the shanty corresponded to its dual use; there were a few rough chairs and a table for guests, and the back wall was covered with rudely fashioned shelves, which were filled with all of the gay coloured and iridescent treasures of the South Seas. There were branches of many-coloured coral, and a thousand different kinds of shells; some were as white as snow, some striped like tigers, some pink, and others that shone with all the colours of the rainbow. Some were infinitesimal; others were huge. Some were formed with gently curving, shimmering surfaces; others were full of jagged corners and edges, thorns and spines. Among the collection were sea horses and sea urchins, and in one particularly lovely mother-of-pearl shell there was a cluster of pearls, not very large or valuable, but quite remarkable as to their shape and colour; a few were entirely black and others were a deep rose. All these beautiful and strange treasures lay in piles on the shelves of this tumble-down little shanty. Along one end of the hut there was a makeshift bar, where a lively business was carried on; especially when the packet boat *Lübeck* or any larger ship was lying in the roads of Apia. At such times the regular clientele was made up of sailors, beachcombers, half-castes and some more or less shopworn South Seas beauties. The better class of white traders, the officials of the German Plantation Society, and especially the higher-ups in Apia's municipal ranks kept a safe distance from the shell shop, and the missionaries took occasion to condemn it in their sermons. But Middy, who was in the flood tide of his sins, was a steady customer; the shell merchant was his good friend, and had staked him to many a free drink when he had been thirsty in return for a little music for the guests. When he had no other shelter the young beachcomber could always sleep at the shell merchant's, on a mat in the corner.

When Middy and old Horncastle came into the shanty they found, besides the proprietor, only one of the usual queer folk one sees in the South Seas. This was a man who, to judge by his accent, must have had an English name once upon a time, but who was now commonly known as Nuku-hiva, after one of the numberless islands which figured in his wild tales. If one believed what this disreputable old gentleman said, he must have at least one brown wife and a raft of children on every island in Polynesia. He loved to tell about them, and did so with great frequency. There was, for example, the story of how, in Fiji, he had espoused, with certain outlandish ceremonies, a wife named Betsy Brownlegs, his eighth. The tale was highly improper, and he had repeated it *ad nauseam*; nevertheless, he began to tell it again the moment Middy and Horncastle came into the shop. As soon as he had served his customers, the half-breed shell merchant retired to his corner behind the bar and began to sleep—audibly. It was terribly close, so the shutters were wide open and through them a bit of the beach was visible and beyond that the grey sea with its ominous-looking white crested waves; the sky had become overcast and a violent thunderstorm seemed imminent. The surf pounded what was left of the wreck of the German cruiser *Adler,* which had come to grief in the treacherous roads of Apia during the memorable storm of March, 1889. Since then this once-powerful battleship, whose guns had often enough played a sinister part in the history of Samoa, had lain out in the the middle of the harbour of Apia like a drowned leviathan, through whose ribs the sea winds swept.

The first distant clap of thunder wakened the shell merchant and roused old Nukuhiva out of the alcoholic daze in which he had been telling his filthy story. He murmured: "The niggers have already begun to shoot! It's Mataafa's men!" Then he laid his unshaven chin on the table and went sound asleep beside his glass of gin.

But Horncastle, connoisseur of the beach and its noises could distinguish between a clap of thunder and a shot from a gun. He issued a pontifical denial of the false statement. To be sure, one had to be prepared for the shooting to begin any time now in Samoa, but as yet the time had not come. On the one side of the bay of Apia, in Mulinuu, lived the King who had been installed by the whites, Malietoa Laupepa. He was old and lacking in energy, besides which he was highly unpopular with his subjects—if you could call these unruly people that. At the other end of the bay, at Malie, entrenched behind palisades, sat Laupepa's rival and cousin, Mataafa, with his followers. They seemed to be bent on an open revolt and prepared for it, although hostilities had not yet begun. In between these two armed camps of the natives lay the only small patch of white civilization on the island of Upolu, the little town of Apia, the warehouses, the beach. Every child knew that Mataafa was presently going to attack Laupepa. People like old Horncastle knew about every rifle, every case of cartridges, which had been purchased by the people of Malie in recent weeks, and from whom. Officially the three Protectorate Powers were behind Laupepa, and the Germans, who had had a well-founded grudge against Mataafa, were especially ardent in their attitude; yet all the unofficial sympathy of the majority, not only of Samoans, but of the resident Englishmen and Americans, was on the side of his rival Mataafa.

"Stevenson has his whole house crammed with guns, damn

his eyes!" hiccoughed old Horncastle. "When Mataafa begins to operate, he will make Stevenson his Field Marshal: that's a fact. He's a great fellow, that Stevenson; he can do a lot more than scribble on paper. He's deep, I tell you, Middy; he's a deep one! But perhaps the Chief Justice will deport him before he gets that far; they don't want him to keep putting in his oar and helping the niggers. Did you see him riding by just now? He was on his way to Malie, to his friend Mataafa; he writes letters for him to Queen Victoria. He does really!"

Outside, the tropical rain crashed down in an uncontrollable, catastrophic flood. The shell merchant rushed to the door to close it quickly, and as he did so he saw a man striding along the beach in the direction of his shanty. To protect himself against the rain, the man had wrapped an old straw mat—goodness knows where he had picked it up—around his body. This helped to keep out some of the flood as he ran, dripping wet and breathless, towards the shop. He splashed through a big puddle, reached the door and came in, abandoning his streaming mat on the threshold. Here was the wolf of their stories, Tusitala himself, whose diabolical machinations had just been the subject of discussion in this saloon, as in every saloon on every beach in the whole of the South Seas. In other words, here was Robert Louis Stevenson, who at this moment appeared to be much more damp than diabolical. He glanced around the shell shop with curiosity.

Contrary to the cocksure opinion of the beach, Stevenson had not been spending the day with the Pretender Mataafa, writing inflammatory letters to Queen Victoria; as a matter of fact, he had not even seen Mataafa for some time. It was true that his presence in Apia on this particular day was connected with Mataafa, but in quite a different way from what Horncastle, with his pothouse political wisdom, surmised. He had ridden into town to make an eleventh-hour attempt at a peaceable settlement between the opposing parties of the chieftains who were on the brink of making a senseless war on each other. To be sure, he looked upon Laupepa as weak and incapable, a mere puppet dressed up by the Great Powers in a grotesque king's uniform, and he looked upon Mataafa as the only hope of the Samoan people. But he did not conclude from these opinions that an armed conflict was desirable or that he was willing to further one, as the beach gossipers believed. On the contrary, his wish was to reconcile the two squabbling cousins, to turn Laupepa's purely nominal control of Samoa into a real rule; and in order to achieve this purpose he was trying to persuade the King to give the much more energetic Mataafa some share in the government. This could be done by one of two methods: he could make Mataafa Viceroy, or he could go through the fiction of adopting him. This would involve complicated and ceremonial preparatory negotiations, and it was Stevenson's idea that they could take place at his house. This would mean, of course, a lot of bother and loss of time, which was not entirely a welcome idea to a hard-working writer. It would entail inviting the chiefs of both parties and their numerous followers to a tremendous feast in Samoan style. It would mean putting before them the traditional drink of kava, with strict adherence to every single detail of the ancient ritual, for without this no negotiations or even friendly social relations could take place in Polynesia. There would have to be the hereditary Talking Men, who inevitably accompany all Samoan High Chiefs, and who indulge in endless orations according to fixed rhetorical forms. Then one might—if one had had the patience to survive thus far through the barbaric and feudal ceremonies of a congress of Samoan High Chiefs—one might quietly slip in a pertinent remark to make these sulking children, who were scrapping about empty titles and mats decorated with heraldic emblems, realize what the real point at issue was: the preserving of peace and the freedom of their people.

Stevenson had no intention of making this attempt at reconciliation behind the backs of the representatives of the Protectorate Powers, or the official advisers of Laupepa. It was for the purpose of bringing his plan to their official knowledge that he had called, on this particular day, on the Swede Cedercrantz ,who had held the office of Chief Justice since the Berlin Convention, and on the Prussian Baron Senfft von Pilsach. Neither of these officials was friendly to Stevenson, but they had listened to him politely and at least raised no objections, although neither of them really welcomed his efforts at mediation. He was now free to send off his invitations to the King and Mataafa; and the prospect of the possibility of serving the ends of peace and, in doing so, of playing an important and glorious role, made him, for the time being, extremely happy. What would Sir George Grey say if his great project should succeed!

After his official calls were over, Stevenson had taken a meal at the hotel and put up his horse Jack, while he went to do various errands about the town. He had come to the shell shop on purpose, because he had heard of this merchant and hoped to pick up some lovely mother-of-pearl bowls for his beloved great hall. On the way he had been overtaken by the storm. It was such a nuisance, and what would Fanny say if he came home with a cold in his head? His raincoat he had, of course, left behind in the hotel. Somewhere he had picked up an old straw mat and made a dash for the shop, thinking, as he ran, of the beautiful speech he would make if he should ever see Sir George Grey again: all about the saving of the Polynesian people through its own efforts and with only the slightest encouragement of good advice on the part of the white friends of the Kanakas. He was just formulating in his mind a few more good phrases that would certainly please Sir George, when he arrived, dripping wet and happy, in the doorway of the shell shop.

He came in, and his good humour radiated throughout the place. Old Horncastle, who had just been holding forth with

78

the silliest kind of beach gossip about Tusitala, turned redder in the face than ever when he saw him. It was a pleasure, said he, and gave R. L. S. such a hearty slap on his emaciated back that he was thrown against the bar. The old drunkard did not do this out of any evil intention; he merely wanted to impress upon his young buddy that he, Horncastle, a brave old British seaman, knew what good manners were and was on cordial terms with the finest gentry. The old beachcomber Nukuhiva roused himself from his stupor long enough to grunt a not-unfriendly greeting to the newcomer, and then went back to his glass. Meantime he considered the question of whether or not to tell the gentleman the famous story of his marriage with Betsy Brownlegs, the Fiji beauty. The shell merchant received his illustrious customer with a subservient grin. Stevenson was thirsty from running and ordered his favorite drink, which was a glass of lemon juice with a dash of gin; then he turned his attention to the shells. He stood in front of the shelves, cigarette in hand, and began to take out pieces which pleased him.

Meantime Middy had remained in the background. The boy was shy and a little hurt that Mr. Stevenson had obviously not recognized him. He had, to be sure, nodded to him when he came in, but he had paid no further attention to him. The young beachcomber did not like this at all; so he quietly put his fiddle up to his chin and prepared to attract attention by playing. He chose for the occasion, in honour of the Scottish author, "Annie Laurie." This fiddler of the beach was quite accustomed to having drunken sailors turn sentimental when he played tunes from their home countries to them. For instance, he knew a certain English air, which, if he began it, would make old Nukuhiva howl; it made him start off on a long story about a certain girl back in Yorkshire, whose favourite song it was. If he were *very* drunk indeed, he would sometimes, under the right conditions, imply that when he left this sweetheart of his youth he had planted a knife in her. But that was like all the rest of Nukuhiva's stories about women; it might or it might not be true.

The Scottish poet was a slight disappointment to Middy because he did not do the expected thing and break into tears at first sound of "Annie Laurie"; he did not even do it when Middy passed on to "Auld Lang Syne," and all the other Scottish melodies he knew. He turned around only once to look at the musician, and aside from that he kept his attention closely riveted, smoking one cigarette after the other, on the shells and corals; he picked up one, then another and, much to the merchant's joy, laid many aside to purchase.

At last he spoke to the fiddler.

"Have you been in the South Seas for some time?" he asked. "Do you like it? Where would you rather be, in Samoa or at home?"

Young Middy was quite elated. He had accomplished what he had secretly set out to do: to arouse a sense of homesickness in this famous man, through the magic of his music. He had been impressed by Stevenson, and now it was up to him to make the gentleman realize that he was speaking to a person of his own kind, that he was a travelling artist in reduced circumstances, and not just an ordinary vagabond.

"Yes, indeed, the climate here is glorious," said the young beachcomber, in such a prim tone and cultivated voice that old Horncastle's eyes popped out of his head. "But sometimes one does have a feeling of longing for the land one has left behind."

Stevenson threw away his cigarette. He is going to invite me to his house, dreamed the young man. I shall play for him and read him my poems. He will . . .

But the hoped-for invitation was not forthcoming. "Your shells are marvellously beautiful," said Stevenson to the merchant. "I'll send for these pieces which I have chosen. I shall need more; please save me any especially fine ones. And corals, too. I am very fond of coral. . . . I think the rain is letting up."

He paid for his drink and left, rather abruptly. He was hardly through the door when old Horncastle, pointing after him, said: "He's off to his old Mataafa!" His parasite, young Middy, felt obliged to laugh at the penetrating remark, but in his heart he was feeling that he had missed and spoiled a great opportunity.

The rain was far from over, so R. L. S. used his old straw mat as an umbrella and hurried over to the hotel. It was foolish not to have waited for the end of the storm, to get soaked through a second time, he thought to himself; but if that fellow had played "Auld Lang Syne" with that awful tremolo once more, I should have had to smash his violin over his head. He probably meant well, of course he did, but . . .

He held the mat over his head to keep from getting wetter than he already was, and at the same time, as he ran along, he tried to find some protection inside himself against the unexpected flood of homesickness which had been loosed in him in such a tactless way. He set himself to thinking about his novel *Catriona,* in which he had painted all the rugged romance of the Scottish Highlands, and revived all the unforgettable memories of the Rising of 1745. This story was already running as a serial in a magazine and was to appear in book form in the autumn.

Catriona: the happy home-coming of an exiled Scot, young David Balfour of Shaw. After so many adventures, so many journeys, so much homesickness . . .

The rain smelled like a good, healthy country rain in the Scottish Highlands, and Robert Louis Stevenson's favourite idea flashed through his mind: in the last analysis, how like his own half-savage Highland Scots these beloved Samoans of his really were! The hero of *Catriona,* the Highland rebel Alan Breck Stewart, must have been quite like Simele, or any other chief in the Mataafa party, all of them defiant clansmen, fanatic in their legitimist loyalty to an hereditary leader.

82

Mataafa! What can be done now to see to it that Mataafa and that senile old Laupepa really become reconciled, and do not just appear to be at peace? Thank goodness, here is the hotel at last! Fanny will be furious when she finds out that I have been running around again in the worst of the storm!

CHAPTER VI

THE FROG KING

ONE day toward the end of April, Stevenson sat, surrounded by manuscripts, in his study on the first floor of his house, Vailima. There were a great many manuscripts in various stages of completion, and their busy author was going through them with the absorption a miser might have in his bank notes. There were the proofs of *Catriona* almost ready for the printer. The first rough version of *Ebb Tide,* a novel of the South Seas, which R. L. S. had written with Lloyd Osbourne, was finished and needed only some revision of details. The other fragments . . .

Will this really make a good book, was the question R. L. S. asked himself for the hundredth time as he fingered the manuscript of *Ebb Tide*? The story, which he had discussed at such length with Lloyd, sometimes seemed quite remarkable to him; it was interesting and at the same time so poorly executed that at times he was tempted to destroy it. In such moments of depression he had entertained the idea of taking Lloyd Osbourne's name off the title page; how could a budding author be allowed to compromise himself to such an extent?

Or was this half-finished book really not so bad but—just different? Just not a real Robert Louis Stevenson book? Was it that some foreign and contradictory element, which went against the grain of his style and his manner of shaping a story, had been introduced, so that it would be better to omit the name of Stevenson from the title page? But who would buy a book by a young beginning writer? And R. L. S. had already used up the royalties paid in advance.

He weighed the manuscript in his hand for a moment as though to establish its intellectual weight. Then he turned, with a slight sigh, to other papers.

There lay the first sheets of the *Records of a Family of Engineers*. This was not a novel. R. L. S. intended it as a monument to his grandfather, a sort of beacon named, too, for his beloved father, Thomas Stevenson, for both of them were lighthouse engineers. Then there were fragments of *St. Ives,* now fairly on the way to completion, and the first sketchy outlines for two great Scottish novels, *Weir of Hermiston* and *The Young Chevalier.*

Nor was that by any means all; there were many more embryo novels and outlines, besides newspaper articles, essays and letters to be written. What a mass of work! Not even Stevenson's favourite literary idols, not Flaubert nor Balzac, had produced half so much at one time. And to think that my trunks are already packed, reflected R. L. S. with a peculiar mixture of pride and bitterness, and labelled "Passenger to Hades."

(A fleeting glance up the crest of Mt. Vaea.)

That is a good line, thought Stevenson, and next time I write home I must bring it in; my trunks are packed! A passenger to Hades.

He laid the manuscripts carefully away, each in its own portfolio.

It is remarkable, he thought to himself, that, with the single exception of *Ebb Tide,* of which I am not the sole author, I have recently been working only on stories laid in a country thousands of miles from the South Seas, in Scotland. While people around here think I am spending all of my time conspiring on behalf of the pretender to the throne, Mataafa, I am really, if the truth were known, much more concerned with the affairs of the Pretender Charlie Stuart.

He had again picked up some sheets of *The Young Chevalier,* whose scene was laid partly in France, partly in Scotland of the eighteenth century, when an interruption came. Stevenson sensed, rather than heard, people coming towards the house. He jumped up, all nerves. What a nuisance! I cannot get any work done in this house! Why doesn't Fanny hold them off, away from me?

He stepped, sulky but nevertheless curious, out onto the broad veranda from which he could overlook the great lawn in front of the house. His cigarette fell from his mouth when he saw who had come out to Vailima to call on him. It was an old Samoan, surrounded by a group of armed men. Four

Kanakas, instead of wearing the usual loin cloth, were dressed in long trousers and jackets of a military cut, both impeccably white. To be sure, the rifles they carried on their shoulders pointed in all four directions of the compass; yet their attitude, on the whole, was decidedly warlike. These were soldiers of the royal bodyguard. Stevenson recognized the old man whom they escorted; it was Malietoa Laupepa, King of the Samoa Archipelago.

A little while ago R. L. S. would not have been astonished by a visit of this sort from the King. Laupepa had been to see him, that is, before his new and much more beautiful house had been built. Besides, Stevenson and the ladies of his household had made frequent visits to the old King and Queen in Mulinuu, and had been received with all the ceremonies due the dignity of such distinguished guests. But all that was before the period when the rivalry between Laupepa and Tusitala's friend Mataafa had become so acrimonious. That the old King should come now, at a time when the whole beach was buzzing with Stevenson's intrigues on behalf of Mataafa, and that he should come of his own accord, unannounced and practically unaccompanied, must be a happy omen. Stevenson's heart beat faster; for a moment his hopes soared. Perhaps Laupepa had come to accept the invitation to discuss matters with Mataafa; perhaps he had realized at last that, without the help of his stalwart and popular cousin, he could never hold the Samoans together and save what remained of their independence—if not real independence, at least some sort of peaceable national existence.

In any case it was extraordinary that Malietoa Laupepa had dispensed with the customary following which was looked upon as essential to any visit of state on the part of a High Chief of Samoa. Even the official "Talking Man," without whom a diplomatic exchange in Samoa was well-nigh unthinkable; even he was missing. Stevenson shaded his eyes with his hand, but all he could distinguish was a guard of four soldiers who were stacking their arms in the shade of a tree and evidently not intending to enter the house. Besides them and Laupepa himself, the only other visible person was a half-naked, very black, fuzzy-headed Kanaka, whom R. L. S. felt he must have seen somewhere before. But that could not be the "Talking Man," because these heralds of Samoan dignitaries are themselves of chieftain rank and always make an appearance of great state. This black man was obviously one of the cannibals from the Solomon Islands, who had been imported against their will to Samoa. They pretended to a knowledge of broken English; so perhaps this "black boy" was brought along as an interpreter.

It occurred to Stevenson that the official "Talking Man" of the house of Vailima, namely Lloyd Osbourne, was also absent; he had, as happened very often of late, ridden into town. And Lloyd was the best interpreter they had at Vailima. R. L. S. himself spoke the current household language with considerable fluency. But he did not know his way around very well in the special High Chief dialect. It was rather uncomfortable, too, to feel that he was speaking like an uncultivated, rude barbarian.

But it could not be helped. Inside the house everything was already in an uproar; the native servants were running around in a state of frenzy. They were probably hurrying to replace their lava-lava aprons with their Sunday livery of which they were so proud. This livery consisted of a white shirt and Highland kilts made of the Royal Stuart tartan.

Robert Louis Stevenson himself hastily slipped on his velvet jacket, which he had hung over the back of a chair while he was working, and he looked around for some shoes, which he never wore in the house; but he could not find any, so he shrugged his shoulders impatiently, and went downstairs in his bare feet to greet his royal guest in the main hall.

Today Malietoa Laupepa, King of Samoa, did not have on his ridiculous gold-braided uniform of a non-existent army, with epaulettes and the broad silk ribbon of a non-existent order; he used this regalia only on occasions when he expected to be photographed. Nevertheless he had come in European attire, like that of his bodyguard. He had trousers and even shoes on; under his gleaming white jacket, however, one could catch a glimpse of one whalebone necklace, and of another longer one made in a more complicated fashion with a quantity of red seeds and little iridescent shells.

King Laupepa had great, wide-open eyes that goggled like frog's eyes at the world, and a long soft moustache, which fell over his full, slightly negroid lips. If he looked like a king at all, it was like the Frog King of the fairy tales. He was old, tired, good-natured and somewhat stupid. Life had brought some extraordinary things to this old Kanaka chieftain. He had achieved the highest honours to which a man of his race and nation could aspire: the title of king, an uncomfortable dress uniform with a gold embroidered collar and epaulettes, a make-believe royal standard which he could fly from his otherwise quite shabby palace, and a right to a salute of a certain number of guns from foreign battleships, which now and then wished to honour him. All this was King Laupepa's and many more regal insignia of various kinds; but he possessed neither any power nor the respect of his people. No one could deny that he was an Alii, a High Chief, of an infinitely long and glorious ancestry traced back to those ancient gods in whom Samoa, officially at least, no longer believed. But there were other chieftains too, his rivals and relatives, Mataafa and Tamasese. By his ancestry, Mataafa especially had an equally valid claim, not to the Samoan throne (which piece of furniture was non-existent), but to the leadership of his little nation. Unfortunately, a few years previously, during the mix-up in Samoan affairs, Mataafa had had the mischance to fall afoul of one of the rival Great Powers, the Germans; that is why they turned against this man who had been their publicly declared favourite, and now supported Laupepa. In those early days things had been quite different; the German consul had even had Laupepa summarily arrested as a disturber of the peace, after a brawl of some kind, and brought aboard one of those strange, unbelievable battleships which the Papalangi have. Aboard the *Albatross* Laupepa was taken first to a foreign land, where all the people were coal black; it was called the Cameroons and belonged to the Germans. But the German Papalangi kept him there only for a short time; then they put him on another ship and took him for a long, long voyage. Then one day they came to a country with white cliffs; and a Samoan prisoner, who stood shivering beside him at the rail, said it was England. But the ship did not stop. It went on until it came to a place called Hamburg, where there was an immense house with a glass roof. There were carriages there; they were not drawn by horses, but by an Aitu, who breathed steam. In one of these enchanted carriages Laupepa had been transported to another city; it was called Bremerhaven, and in its harbour lay ships, which plied from Germany to Samoa.

Why was he taken from Samoa to Bremerhaven and put aboard a ship which would bring him back to the South Seas? Poor Laupepa never discovered. At first he was very cold; then they came to the Red Sea he had heard so much about from the missionaries when he was a boy. But the sea was not at all red, and there were no traces to be found either of the wicked Pharaoh or of Moses. But it was warmer—in fact it grew hot—and Laupepa, who had nearly died of homesickness in Germany, was very happy because it seemed certain that he was going home. Along the coasts and on the islands they passed, the coco palms waved gayly to him. But then the ship stopped—who can ever understand the Papalangi—at the island of Jaluit, in the Marshall Archipelago, which is very far from Samoa; on this strange and unfriendly island Laupepa was compelled to live as a prisoner for many months. To be sure, there were coco palms there, but no breadfruit or taro. Even if his German gaolers did give him good ship's hardtack and tea, and tinned meats, too, still it was no life one could live indefinitely; Laupepa became very sad and began to long for death.

But then one day the Papalangi brought him back to Samoa to set him free and allow him to be restored to his old-time rank and possessions. They did all this with as apparently little real reason as they had shown in carrying him off. For what had he ever done to them?

Then the struggle had been resumed with his cousins, Mataafa and Tamasese; and suddenly the Germans became angry at Mataafa and all three consuls, the German, American and British, said: The Samoans must make a free choice of their king and we decree that from now on Malietoa Laupepa is king.

And from then on he was *Tupu o Samoa,* King of all Samoa.

He no longer lived in Apia (he had no say there; the foreigners ruled the town), but out on the peninsula of Mulinuu. He took orders from the foreign consuls, from the Chief Justice Cedercrantz, from the President of the Municipality Senfft von Pilsach, from the missionaries and from the German Plantation Society. Sometimes the Papalangi were friendly, and sometimes they stormed at the poor, timid, old Frog King. His subjects paid him no taxes; to do that never even occurred to them. Besides, although he was the recognized king, over across the bay at Malie sat Mataafa, surrounded by armed followers, who laid claim to Laupepa's titles under the pretext that he was the favored choice of the Samoan people, elected according to the stipulations of the Berlin Treaty, which guaranteed them this right.

Poor Laupepa found all this rather hard to grasp. One could see from the bewildered look in his frog eyes that he did not really understand the world and the white peoples.

The household of Vailima had been thrown into a certain degree of confusion by the unexpected arrival of His Samoan Majesty. From the talk that was flying around, Stevenson concluded that Fanny was in the house but not yet dressed, and that she was keeping the servants on the run with a hundred errands. He himself was not at all overwhelmed by the honour of the royal visit, and he went forward to greet Laupepa on the threshold of the hall with all the calm of a grand seigneur, who takes for granted the comings and goings of kings and knows how to receive one as a guest.

Inside himself he was delighted because, at the very last moment, the Samoan expression "afionga," which means "Majesty," had come to his mind. He remembered it with amused pride, because Mataafa had once addressed him that way in a letter.

His Majesty Laupepa, on entering, asked after the health of His Excellency, the High Chief Tusitala. He used the expression, "Lana Susunga"—Your Excellency. They shook hands, whereupon Laupepa quite naïvely looked around the famous hall, which he had never seen before and which aroused his curiosity. He was especially attracted to the two gift Burmese statues of Buddha, which stood on either side of the foot of the staircase. Then he noticed the great oak bookcase, on top of which, somewhat in the background, stood a plaster cast of a statue by Auguste Rodin, a youth and a maid in an embrace. Several of the missionaries had made objections to these nude figures, and the King had heard about the impropriety of this work of art in Tusitala's house. He would have liked to get a closer view of it, but first, of course, he must seat himself with formal dignity on the Victorian thronelike overstuffed armchair in the hall. At his feet crouched the black boy he had brought with him as interpreter.

During all the preliminary ceremonial exchange of greetings, followed by barely comprehensible but nevertheless lengthy translation into the most horrible pidgin English, Malietoa Laupepa went on with his furtive but careful scrutiny of Tusitala's house, which must have seemed to him like some palace out of the Arabian Nights. In one corner of the hall stood the great iron safe. Laupepa had heard that it was in this very box that Tusitala kept, along with other fabulous treasures, the famous little bottle with the imp in it. Naturally it was not proper to show too much curiosity at this point; the initial ceremonies were as yet far from over. So His Majesty Laupepa inquired once more about the state of health of His Excellency, the High Chief. Stevenson grasped the drift of the question and could have replied himself, but he preferred to let the Melanesian savage, who reeked of sweat and rancid cocoa butter, do the interpreting because he was fearful of making some slip in etiquette, some ridiculous grammatical error in the High Chief dialect, the flowery terms of which were well-nigh sacred. He returned the proper thanks for the inquiry, offered His Majesty a Havana cigar, lighted up a cigarette himself and sat back to wait for his guest to set forth the reasons for his unusual visit, Laupepa, who was obviously embarrassed, talked vaguely of being on a trip from Mulinuu to this part of the coast; he had taken the opportunity, in passing by, of presenting his greetings to Tusitala. . . .

When, however, Stevenson excused his wife's absence and said that she would presently appear to offer their illustrious guest the hospitality of the house of Vailima, the King decided to speak. He had a healthy respect for the Mistress Aolele, and he preferred to discuss things with Tusitala while they were alone. For he had something highly unpleasant to say, which would be a bitter disappointment to Stevenson. He had decided to decline Tusitala's offer to arrange a meeting of reconciliation. He was aware, he said, that Tusitala's intentions were of the best, and that is why he wished to accompany his regretful rejection of the plan with a personal expression of his esteem for the white friend of the Samoans. . . .

This was followed by a rather lengthy, diplomatic discourse which the grinning cannibal, at the King's feet, was utterly incapable of translating exactly, and which Stevenson could follow only with a great effort. He spoke of earlier negotiations in which the proposal had been made that he, Malietoa Laupepa, adopt the rebellious Mataafa in order to bring about peace. There had been no question, naturally, of Mataafa's adoption as a son; that would have given this ambitious man too many prerogatives. The idea was that the adoption should take place on a peculiarly Samoan basis, by which the person adopted, even if he were a man, received the rank and place of a daughter in the house of the adopter. Mataafa had been too proud, a year ago, to accept this compromise, and now Laupepa, for his part, rejected the idea of accepting so unruly a daughter.

The rest was a maze of elaborate High Chief expressions; Robert Louis Stevenson thought he caught a reference to the five territorial titles, which in their collective total represent the basis of the power of the King of Samoa; then he heard

Laupepa speak of "fine mats," yes, mats artfully interwoven with the feathers of birds, which, as Stevenson knew very well, in the South Seas took place of royal robes, royal standards and royal treasure. At this point it was clear either that Mataafa had already committed, or was about to commit, some unforgiveable crime; he could not precisely understand.

But the trend of all these childish complaints was obvious enough to the long-suffering listener, as he sat opposite the old man who looked more and more like a croaking frog; some intrigues or other uncontrollable influences were working against the effort at reconciliation. It was evident, too, that this good-for-nothing puppet king was dangling helplessly and without any will of his own at the end of strings manipulated by some hidden hand; nor would it do any good to talk reason to the old man and try to make him understand that it was not a question of mouldy old mats and feudal titles, but of the very existence of the whole people of Samoa. Stevenson thought, with a pang, of Mataafa who was no longer young either—in fact, an ignorant old Kanaka—but how much wiser, more manly, a born statesman and king! If there were anyone capable of saving Samoa, it was he.

Suddenly Stevenson flew into a rage against this childish, senile weakling who had come in and disturbed his work; and immediately he felt a sense of relief. In the weeks to come, instead of sitting around with Samoan chieftains drinking kava and listening to endless ceremonial rhetoric, he would have time for his own writing. Perhaps he could make some real headway with his *Weir of Hermiston!*

Fanny's somewhat vigorous and explosive entrance, coupled with her greetings—in a sort of baby talk which she liked to think the Samoans understood—put an end to a situation which was rapidly becoming impossible. The great wooden kava bowl, the pride of the house of Vailima, was carried in, and all serious conversation was immediately abandoned.

The inevitable ceremony of drinking kava was performed. Perhaps it was lacking in some of the intricacies of true etiquette required by the High Chief code, but it was carried through with a satisfactory degree of dignity. This was not the "royal" kava rite which Stevenson had shown to his friend, the wife of Lord Jersey, Governor General of South Australia, in the house of Mataafa. There it had been performed with trained heralds, who had called the names and titles of the guests in precise order of precedence, and who had recited about a thousand drink rituals. Today in Vailima the Talking Man was absent; besides, in place of the customary "Taupò," the village vestal who ordinarily served the kava on ceremonious occasions, Fanny herself, with her firm, brown, unceremonious hands, prepared the opaque liquid.

The polished coco-shell bowl with the kava (which contains no alcohol and does not taste very good, but is a wonderful thirst-quencher and clears the brain in a remarkable way) was carried by Tusitala, the High Chief himself, to the

King's chair. He presented it with a short speech, in which he referred ungrammatically but very politely to the five feudal titles of his highborn guest and addressed him several times as "Lana afionga," Your Majesty. Then Henry Simele, who had meantime appeared, brought a second bowl to Tusitala. Simele did not wear the combination Samoan, Highland-plaid livery of the house of Vailima; as a chieftain in his own right he was dressed all in white. In presenting the drink he announced Tusitala's rank and title in ringing tones and used the attribute "Susunga," Excellency. It was only after that, although she was in her own house, that Fanny was allowed to have the third bowl. Even this was a special favour and exception because, strictly speaking, even as the wife of a chieftain she had no right to drink kava with the men. Simele's manner made this very clear, even without any words, when he fetched a shell dish of kava from the great bowl and offered it to her with a certain condescension.

Although R. L. S. was forming his conventional phrases with a smiling mouth, still Fanny realized that something had angered him. But, of course, the royal visitor must be entertained with a cordiality in keeping with their hospitality. The native servants and members of the household came into the hall, some on practically threadbare pretexts. Among them were members of the King's party and also followers of Mataafa; all, however, were proud of being recipients of the honour of the royal visit, and every one of them did his best to make an impression with his Stuart plaid loincloth and his smart white shirt. The cook Talolo, Sosimo, Jopu and Sina, Talolo's fifteen-year-old wife, came in bringing fruits and refreshments of all sorts. King Laupepa eagerly tasted the canned fruit, which, because it came all the way from California in tin cans, was much more rare and to be appreciated than all the marvellous fruits of Samoa. But his main interest lay in the fabulously splendid hall itself in which he was seated. He studied every picture on the wall. One of them attracted him particularly; it was of the Lighthouse of Skerryvore, built by Stevenson's grandfather on the coast of Scotland. King Laupepa had seen lighthouses on his involuntary journey to Europe, but he had not known then what their purpose was.

His bushy white eyebrows went up a fraction when, in one corner of the room, he saw a gunrack, with a shotgun in it. Lloyd had carried the other gun, which usually stood beside it, over to his cottage. The rumours which were rife along the beach must have reached King Laupepa; he looked around for the hundreds of rifles which Tusitala, according to hearsay, was supposed to have in his house. As a matter of fact, Stevenson had had a dream of heroic proportions about how he would defend his house if anyone came to attack it. The "anyone" of his dream could only be King Malietoa Laupepa, who now was sitting there in such friendly fashion, engaged in consuming a California peach. The arms, numbering six in all, with which R. L. S. had expected to defend himself against this man, had not even been ordered; but Laupepa

would not have believed this even if Tusitala had told him
so on oath. The old gentleman said nothing about rifles, but
he gave away the fact that arms were on his mind when he
began, out of a clear sky, to talk about revolvers. He re-
marked lightly, and opened his frog eyes wide as he did so,
that he did not own a revolver, that he would like to have
one; would they be very expensive if he ordered one from
Beletania? The King of Samoa, who was obliged to pay
high monthly salaries in cash to his white "advisers," had
himself an income of something less than a hundred dollars
a month in cash, so he could not easily indulge in any ex-
travagance.

When Stevenson heard his guest express a wish which he
was in a position to gratify, he was delighted; he had been
racking his brain and could not think of a suitable present to
offer to Laupepa at the conclusion of his call. He jumped up
and went to his iron safe.

The thought that flashed through the old Kanaka's head
was: Tusitala has gone to get the bottle with the imp in it!
And although he was a brave warrior, who had a number of
enemies' heads to his personal credit, he was alarmed. But it
was rather a pleasant chill which ran down his spine; on the
one hand Laupepa was afraid of the magic bottle, and on
the other he was keen to see the little Aitu who had made
Tusitala so boundlessly rich and happy. So, in defiance of
all etiquette, he rose abruptly from his chair and followed

the master of the house over to his safe. Tusitala smiled fleetingly; he was amused, but at the same time he gave his wife a glance which showed he was also annoyed. It had become a usual thing to have his Samoan guests, under a thousand different pretexts, attempt to see the inside of his safe because the fabulous bottle with the imp was supposed to be kept there. By now this game, which R. L. S. had thought so funny in the beginning, had begun to pall. Nevertheless, he opened the safe far enough to give the dusky king a clear view of the contents; there were some papers, a bundle of banknotes (not very large), a few silver coins, and otherwise only the revolver which he intended to bestow upon his guest.

This Stevenson took out; then he closed the safe and came back to the table. "Give me the revolver," said Fanny; "I will show the King how it works." The truth of the matter was that although R. L. S. was better at dreaming heroic dreams, Fanny, who had lived in gold miners' camps in California, was better at handling dangerous weapons than her husband. But he felt King Laupepa's eyes on him and he blushed. "I must first take the cartridges out," he replied, rather irritably. "The revolver is loaded, you know." Then, to demonstrate his masculine coolness and prudence, he broke the revolver, took out the cartridges and stuck them in his pocket. Suddenly it occurred to him: "Perhaps I shall be shot with this very revolver! Perhaps I am giving this fellow a weapon with which he will kill Mataafa!" But it was too late; he could not take back his present. R. L. S. held the beautiful, shiny revolver rather nervously in his hand for a few moments; then he turned it over to Fanny to show the King how it functioned. The latter was as pleased as a child at Christmas. He peeked into the barrel of the revolver with his near-sighted frog eyes, as though to see what went on in the magic tube. He wanted Fanny to show him how to cock it. As the trigger was hard to pull, she had to press it several times—and then some mysterious instinct in the vivid nature of this woman gave a warning. Instead of pressing the trigger for the fifth time, she broke the revolver, without really knowing why she did it, and looked into the fifth chamber, which was the next one in rotation.

In the chamber there was a loaded cartridge. Stevenson, in his preoccupation with his own thoughts, had forgotten to take it out; and if Fanny had pressed the trigger once more it would undoubtedly have meant the end of King Malietoa Laupepa. His head was only a few inches from the mouth of the revolver, and he had been staring right into it.

A voice clamoured inside of Robert Louis Stevenson: "I did not mean to kill him!"

Perhaps the voice protested a little too loudly. What do we know of our unconscious desires, and of the actions which they impel? Naturally, R. L. S., a British gentleman, a civilized being, and a poet, had not intended to murder his guest. Nevertheless his fingers had, unwillingly of course, touched

103

the fateful cartridge and then left it in, while his conscious will had intended carefully to remove them all.

Fanny Stevenson's face turned quite grey—she had too dark a skin to turn white—and her trembling hand laid the ill-omened revolver on the table. For once in her life she was entirely unnerved. She looked at her husband and saw that he was trembling all over.

The only one of the three completely unmoved was the man whose blood might now be flowing over the festively decorated table, King Laupepa. He might look like a frog and he might not be a great monarch or even a wise man; but he was an Alii Sili, a Polynesian chieftain of highest rank, whose ancient blood derives from the fierce old gods of the South Seas; it would take more than a bit of death to frighten this old Frog King. Perhaps he had not even realized the danger he had just escaped. He opened his frog eyes a little wider and his mouth gaped; but the cause of his excitement might well have been the extraordinary behavior of Tusitala and his wife. If, however, the old gentleman had understood the situation aright, then he had conducted himself in a manly and noble way, well worthy of his blood.

Fanny's attempt to soothe him with a flood of baby talk and to ask for forgiveness he cut short with a right royal gesture. He picked the revolver up off the table and stuck it coolly into his pocket, all the while expressing his gratitude for his gorgeous and valuable present from his friend Tusitala with the most ceremonial expressions in High Chief dialect. The black interpreter, who had watched the whole scene in apparently uncomprehending silence, did his best to translate the speech of thanks; but Robert Louis Stevenson, who was still dazed and bewildered, had understood it very well.

The old King took his departure as if nothing had happened. The Samoan servants thronged the doorway to get a last glimpse of Laupepa. In front of the house the four members of the bodyguard picked themselves up lazily off the lawn, placed their royal master in the centre of the cortege and shouldered their guns so that their barrels pointed in all four directions of the compass.

King Malietoa Laupepa called out: "Talofa, Tusitala," My love to you, Teller of Tales! He waved once more as he moved away. As Robert Louis Stevenson returned the greeting, "My love is yours," he thought to himself, rather bitterly: "There goes perhaps the last chance to put an end to the civil war in Samoa!"

Fanny stood on the threshold and looked after the King: "If I had not suddenly had the feeling that you had not taken all of the cartridges out, that man would be dead now, and probably we should be too. No one would have believed that we did not murder the silly old man intentionally."

Stevenson's hand still trembled as he lighted a cigarette. "Yes, he would be dead now," he said, and his smile was somewhat forced when he added, "and we should probably

105

be dead as well, or else we should be preparing to flee from Vailima under cover of night and mist—and Mataafa would be the unquestioned King of Samoa."

He suddenly began to cough violently. The excitement had been too much for him.

It was an uneasy Fanny who led him back into the house. She screamed at a servant to ask if Lloyd was not around. Under his handkerchief, which was rapidly turning red, R. L. S. thought: "Yes, where is Lloyd? I wish I could talk to a man now. Where can Lloyd be?"

Back in his bedroom he looked up to the crest of Mt. Vaea:

There is already too much death in this house. It would have been strange if I had killed a man. No, no, that is one thing I certainly have never meant to do!

CHAPTER VII

TEMPTATION

BY the end of June, 1893, there seemed to be no way to avoid civil war between Mataafa and Laupepa.

Though it is far from being as sanguinary as in civilized countries, war, even in uncivilized parts, is a gruesome and bloody business.

In the wars in the South Seas before the whites mixed in with their battleships, cannon, troop landings, and peace-making diplomats in the conflicts among the islanders, the killing of enemies did not play the principal part. They did engage in it, of course, but the main point consisted of certain warlike ceremonies, dances and chants before the battle, the winning of valuable trophies during the battle, and great ceremonial celebrations afterwards. Unfortunately, in some quarters, and especially in Samoa, these trophies, around which the war was waged, consisted of heads of dead enemies; if it were not necessary to cut them off and show them in traditional fashion at the victory celebration, no blood would flow in a war in Samoa, or at any rate very little. The method of blowing up whole columns of troops, of blasting villages of old people, women and children with bullets, hand grenades and bombs, was something which the champions of western culture had to teach to the warriors of Polynesia; they had been brought up to think that war was a question of individual courage and subsequent boasting.

In Vailima the first sign of imminent hostilities was noted when all the red handkerchiefs in the stores in the surrounding villages were bought up. A turkey red cotton cloth bound around the head of a doughty warrior was the uniform of the royal Samoan army, whereas the partisans of Mataafa could be recognized merely by the lack of the red handkerchiefs. Both sides covered themselves with war paint before they went into battle; they used soot to paint black beards on their faces. This made them look extremely martial and was calculated to terrify the enemy.

This was the first step, but much more dreadful things were to come. In the native villages the spreaders of war propaganda made their appearance; these were the hereditary "Talking Men" whose life job was Samoan politics. They carried the beautifully carved batons of their office; and soon after their arrival in a village the war fever would rise to the boiling point. Great kava feasts were arranged, to which Talking Men of both parties, still on fairly peaceful terms, were invited; and where they held forth against each other in heated, though lengthy, debates full of all the traditional flourishes. In this way, the village chieftains—whose Talking Men also joined in the discussion—were obliged to declare themselves either for the King or for the rebel Mataafa. Soon small groups of either party began to cluster at given rallying points to the accompanying warlike din of drums, trumpets and pipes. The mobilization was almost all-inclusive; even Vailima was obliged to send at least a few of Tusitala's servants, workers and retainers into the field, richly provisioned for the war with fruit and kava root. Often two friends would leave together, one for Mataafa's, the other for Laupepa's camp. They would go laughing and chatting along a bit of the road together, each with his weapons and, if possible, with his wife, who carried his provender and arms.

It went very much against the grain with Tusitala to see his Samoan children divided into opposing camps, but he could do nothing to avert the bloody clash. A man should never fail to do the duty his inheritance has laid on him. Even Tusitala must have realized that, for, after all, he was a Scot and knew how a clansman must bear himself.

While all this was going on in the interior, the beach at Apia was in a turmoil of mostly wild and always changing rumours. One of them was to the effect that it was the royal intention to burn Vailima, that fortified stronghold of Mataafa's partisans, to the ground and capture Tusitala's head as a trophy. Yet although isolated bands of wild-looking warriors, with blackened faces and bristling weapons, showed themselves at Vailima and undoubtedly caused a sensation among the Samoans left at home, still it never occurred to

anyone to be afraid of violent attacks. All the natives, even
the followers of Laupepa, spoke of Tusitala with the deepest
respect and affection, and not so much as a banana was taken
from the stem on the Vailima plantation without his permission.

On the twenty-eighth of June it rained very hard and
R. L. S., who dreaded any slightest cold, should really have
stayed at home. But he was nervous and restless, incapable of
doing a single stroke of work; the wild rumours pouring in
from Apia were too disturbing. One rumour had it that King
Laupepa had just died; another said he was alive but had
fled from the royal residence at Mulinuu; then they said the
Germans had betrayed him, and gone over to Mataafa. Although Louis knew this was all pure nonsense, nevertheless
he was restless at home. After luncheon his cousin Graham
Balfour, who had been visiting in Vailima for several weeks,
offered, much to Fanny's relief, to ride into town with him.

Graham Balfour, one of the Balfours of Pilrig, was a close
relative of Louis on his mother's side. He was an enormously
tall Scotsman, addicted to sea adventures and ethnography,
and had been travelling for some time around the South
Seas, mostly in incredibly small boats, which took him to
unknown islands. Until he landed in Apia one day in the
previous August, Stevenson had not known him personally;
they had never happened to meet before. On that occasion
Stevenson and Fanny had met him in the harbour and taken

him along with them. At home R. L. S., as was his custom, immediately took off his shoes and went barefoot. The stranger, his cousin, immediately followed suit.

"He is a fool like the rest of us," said Stevenson with deep satisfaction, and the two cousins became something which cousins rarely are, good friends. From then on Graham made Vailima his headquarters as he came and went on his mad journeys in the South Seas. Stevenson's Samoans grew to be very fond of this lank, phlegmatic, manly person. As they could not pronounce the name of Graham, they usually called him Palema.

The two cousins rode off in a downpour at about one o'clock. Stevenson was, as usual, mounted on Jack, his favourite horse. They had been obliged to find an exceptionally high horse for Graham, because of his long legs. They arrived without incident in Apia; the little town looked like an anthill in uproar. Every person they met had a mass of news to tell; actually they knew nothing except that drums had been heard in the distance during the night. As they rode along, R. L. S. and Graham heard excited reports of bloody battles which were supposed already to have taken place; whole provinces were said to have risen; frightful atrocities had been committed at unidentifiable places; this or that famous chieftain had been seen, according to these rumours, fighting on one side or the other, if not on both. In short, they were unable to get at the truth of the matter, even when

111

they called on a Scotsman, who bore the proud title of "Secretary of State" of Samoa, and who would have been glad to tell his countrymen anything he knew; but he knew nothing.

Their journey of investigation finally brought them to the edge of the town.

"Well, what about it?" said R. L. S. to his cousin, with a slightly forced laugh. "Shall we ride on for a bit toward Malie? Mataafa's outposts should be at the ford. Perhaps we can find out there what is going on."

Graham Balfour just nodded his head and said nothing.

They rode on until they came to the village of Vaimusu. The Samoan houses, which look like beehives anyway, were as full as beehives and humming with noise. There were many men about, but none of them appeared to be armed. A bit farther on they came to a river, which emptied into the sea at this point; the ford here was much used. Robert Louis Stevenson rode swiftly through the shallow water. His cousin followed him with much less impetuosity.

Over on the other side there was war. Stevenson's brave boyish heart dropped a beat when he saw Mataafa's first sentries. They were a group of young natives, sitting on the bank of the river peaceably laughing and chatting, enjoying the bit of sunlight that was just breaking through a rainbow. These young warriors were girded with well-filled cartridge belts, and in their hands they held shiny new Winchester rifles.

Stevenson's voice rang with unusual solemnity as he cried loudly: "Talofa!" At first the commanding officer of the outpost returned the greeting in a friendly way. "Talofa, Tusitala!" Then it suddenly occurred to him why he was there, and he asked in a stiff, military tone, what were their names and where were they going.

"To Faamuina's," said R. L. S., and they were allowed to pass.

"We are inside of Mataafa's lines," said Stevenson in a rather significant tone to his cousin. The tall Scot nodded briefly, but it was evident that he was enjoying the adventure. He was "a fool like the rest of us" and ready for any bold escapade.

They rode on. Across their path lay a European house belonging to a Chinese. To show that he was neutral and had nothing to do with the war, he had hoisted a huge white flag over his house. On it were Chinese characters which presumably gave further proof of his neutrality. Nevertheless, his veranda was swarming with armed Samoans, who were standing around in proud attitudes, leaning on their Winchester rifles; the naked upper part of their bodies gleamed with oil. Lovely Samoan girls, with garlands of flowers on their necks, stood near the men and gazed at them with admiration. As Tusitala and his cousin Palema rode slowly by, the girls waved to them laughingly and called out that they ought to stop for a rest. But what Stevenson had seen of the

113

war up to this point had only whetted his appetite and made him want to ride on deeper, much deeper, into the adventure.

Just before they reached Faamuina's village, they saw a detachment of warriors on the march. With a pounding heart R. L. S. reined in his horse and looked at these men who were on their way into a real war; there were ten or twelve of them, with blackened faces, their cartridge belts buckled around their carefully oiled, bronze torsos, and their new and shiny rifles, fresh from the store, slung across their strong shoulders. A bugler blew some military signal, without much art in his performance. These warriors did not march in step. They walked along freely and proudly, and on their faces was an expression of courage and joy.

By this time the rain had ceased entirely, and a good strong smell of dampness rose. Between the doorposts of the houses set around the grassy village commons, the rain blinds had been rolled up so that the breeze could blow through. This made it possible to see right through the houses, and they were all full of armed men. Inside the great council hut, which every Samoan village contains, a solemn conclave was in session. In the open doorway it was easy to recognize the hereditary spokesman; his back was turned to his audience, which was seated on the ground around the posts, as he hurled his grievances, his call to arms, his exhortations, whatever they might be, out into the open air of the whole wide world. Long after the two cousins had ridden by, they could still hear the rising and falling rhythm of his great oration.

114

The house of old Faamuina, who for some time had been on terms of great hospitability with Tusitala, stood on a breezy height above the village commons. It was the roomy house of a High Chief, not one of the round huts of the ordinary folk, but oval, in the shape of an inverted boat. The important part of the structure was three substantial pillars placed in the centre. They carried the roof, which looked like a melon cut in half, or the hull of a boat, and which was a marvel of perfect weaving. A kind of cage had been framed out of rafters of breadfruit wood. Between these bars had been woven a close matting of reeds. In this basketry in turn had been carefully interwoven long, dried sugar-cane leaves. The walls were really only made of a loose framework held in place by a few stronger posts; on the weather side were straw blinds to let down. The floor was carefully paved with pebbles over which beautifully woven mats were laid.

Such was Faamuina's house, a house worth seeing in Samoa.

As soon as the two riders had been seen and recognized, a little chocolate-colored boy, almost entirely naked, ran out to take their horses when they dismounted.

Stevenson and Graham Balfour went inside. This house was also full of people. Besides Faamuina and his portly consort Pelepa, three other chieftains of lesser rank were present, together with a number of their followers who, out of respect, did not dare to stand up. One must never stand before great lords in the South Seas; one crouches at their feet.

Stevenson's memory of old Faamuina was quite different; he remembered him as gigantically tall and massively built, but somewhat lame and senile. On this occasion he still limped heavily, but he seemed to have renewed his youth, for he was much more agile and as gay as a boy. It was wonderful to see what a beneficent effect a war, or, rather, just the hope of a war, could have on this descendant of untold generations of warriors. Faamuina greeted his guests with great joy as he exchanged significant glances with the other chieftains. Tusitala's arrival in the midst of Mataafa's partisans aroused great hopes. The master of the house ordered a bowl of kava to be prepared so that he could toast his guests; they sent at once for the Taupò, the maid of honour who officiates at all ceremonies and who enjoys in a Samoan village all the privileges of a vestal virgin in ancient Rome.

But R. L. S. made a hasty move to check the well-meaning enthusiasm of the chieftain. He had just dropped in as he was riding by, to chat for a few minutes with his friends and to inquire about Faamuina's and Pelepa's health. He offered cigarettes to all the men and expressed sincere regret that this time he could not stay long enough to partake of kava.

When Faamuina began to speak of the Taupò, the painful realization had swept over Robert Louis Stevenson that participation in a proper kava drinking in Samoa was bound up with all sorts of ceremonies and speeches which, under the then existing conditions, could not but be a warlike occasion involving political significance. How could these war-

116

riors in Mataafa's camp offer the coco shell of kava to Tusitala other than with the sonorous proclamation of the herald that he, Tusitala, had come as a friend, an ally, perhaps even a companion in arms of King Mataafa?

Like some fiery horse who suddenly balks on the edge of a deep ditch, and shies away, Robert Louis Stevenson shrank from this little ceremony which might commit him irretrievably to a line of conduct which would turn his whole life in some entirely different direction. As he sat crouched on the clean floor of Faamuina's house, neatly inlaid with pebbles, and the smoke rose to the bowl-shaped roof from the cigarette in his hand, it occurred to him that here among the excited dusky South Sea warriors, armed to the teeth, he was in a situation parallel to the one he had planned for his novel, *Weir of Hermiston.* In it there were four gaunt Scottish shepherds sitting in a hut which reeked of smoke from the peat fire, plotting a campaign of revenge against the enemy of their house. He could almost smell the peat, although he knew it was only the coconut oil with which the Samoan warriors were dripping. It roused in the exile a fierce sense of longing for the lonely moors of Scotland and for the hardy, cool, bold Scotsmen:

"Auld, auld Elliots, dour, bauld Elliots of old. . . ."

Yes, it was a real wave of homesickness for the Scotland of his dreams, for the people in his books still unwritten, for the Scottish shepherd by the name of Elliot whom he had created, and who, he suddenly felt, was much more real,

117

more actual and closer to his heart than all these tattooed savages.

Indeed, how had he come there, and to what purpose? He would probably not have been able to account for it himself, but it was really the thought of his book, *Weir of Hermiston,* which he was determined to finish before he died, that caused him all of a sudden to jump up and say to his cousin Graham, or rather to yell at him with unnecessary loudness:

"Come, Graham, we must be riding home now!"

The old chieftain Faamuina, his wife Pelepa and their household looked questioningly at one another. How incalculable, how difficult to understand, were even the best of the Papalangi! To them it had seemed so logical, so much a matter of course, that Tusitala should be on his way to Mataafa's headquarters in Malie, that he and Pelema should join Mataafa and fight on his side against Laupepa. And now, these ill-behaved creatures, without even having drunk any kava, were noisily calling for their horses and riding back to Vailima! What could such conduct portend?

Stevenson swung himself into his saddle without the proffered help of a Samoan warrior who had hastened over to assist him. He had barely mounted when Jack leaped backwards; the horse had been scared by a man with a blackened face who had jumped precipitately out of a flower-laden hibiscus bush in front of the house. The same man, for no known reason, had then proceeded suddenly to execute a series of somersaults and handsprings, with the result that his loincloth of gleaming Tapa fibre fell down over his painted and grinning savage face and revealed his naked legs. These were tattooed all over with marvellously intricate geometric designs and fern pattern arabesques. A nearsighted person might have thought that this savage warrior had on some strangely embroidered blue trousers; actually it was the skin on his loins and hips, which had been covered with wierd, mysterious symbols to the accompaniment of ancient magic rites. And that was what this Samoan brave wanted to show to the two Papalangis.

At the very moment when this grotesque and fear-inspiring savage was performing his barbaric somersaults in front of the house of the chieftain Faamuina, perhaps the further destiny of that highly cultivated European, the writer Robert Louis Stevenson, was being decided.

He went back to Vailima with his cousin Graham Balfour, whose thoroughgoing Scottishness was such a steadying comfort at that moment. Nothing of note occurred on the way home except that R. L. S., too much absorbed in his own thoughts, tried to take an unfamiliar short cut near one of the coco palm plantations, and lost his way in the high tropical grass. A bad slip almost resulted in a serious fall; perhaps it was some feeling within him which was trying to prevent his going back home. Just at the end a heavy shower overtook them, and they arrived home around six o'clock wringing wet. This gave Fanny the opportunity to cover up, in the guise of a gentle scolding, the fears she had been suffering. Louis would catch his death yet in weather like that!

But what did Robert Louis Stevenson care about death and a cold today? He had been in the saddle for five hours and he should have been tired. Yet he had never in all his life felt so lighthearted, so young. As he expressed it, a war horse was neighing inside him.

During supper he gave a lively description of the armed sentries at the ford, of the savage warrior who did somersaults and turned his tattooed rump to the world and to his enemies. Stevenson also said that if he had ridden only a few miles farther on he would have reached Mataafa's headquarters at Malie. There, if he had wished it, yes, he, the invalid writer of books, Robert Louis Stevenson, he would have found an army of brave, brown men who would undoubtedly have received him with open arms. It would have been no trick at all to put himself at their head, march on Apia, take the Chief Justice Cedercrantz prisoner, and overthrow the Frog King Laupepa himself in Mulinuu.

"I could have done it all so easily," he boasted like an excited boy. "And perhaps I shall do it tomorrow. I have always known that I was really born to be a soldier. And now that war has come close to me for the first time . . ."

The members of the family sat around the supper table, which was laden with excellent foods. Palema was silent and unmoved. Fanny watched her husband with half-closed eyes, much as a mother might in listening to her big boy making up stories; her manner was tender, slightly ironic, and yet a little credulous too.

Isobel Strong joined in with her usual vigor: "Oh yes, Lou! We really must do that. We'll ride down tomorrow again to Mataafa's outposts. You will take me along, won't you? I should so like to sketch those warriors at the ford. Do say yes, Lou!"

Robert Louis Stevenson assented in an absent-minded way, but his looks were on Lloyd Osbourne, who sat silent at his place with his spectacled eyes fastened on the tablecloth.

Stevenson got up. "Don't tell me you are going to work now?" said Fanny. "Aren't you tired?"

"I am going into the soldiers' room for a bit," said R. L. S. and looked at Lloyd. But Lloyd did not budge.

The soldiers' room was near Stevenson's study and was so called because it contained a quantity of lead soldiers. Many of them had belonged to Lloyd Osbourne as far back as when he was a little boy in Davos. The present titular owner of the lead soldier army was Lloyd's nephew, Austin Strong, Isobel's little son who at this time was away in school in San Francisco. It was a shame, because so many exciting things were happening now at home, in his dearly loved Samoa. Austin heard about these doings only through the fascinating letters which his Uncle Louis, who was really his step-grandfather, addressed to him as "The Overseer," or "Respected

121

Hopkins," or "My dear Hutchinson." Yet no matter how many gay and interesting things he reported in these letters, Uncle Louis never said a word about the fact that recently he had been spending more time in the soldiers' room playing with Austin's lead soldiers. Naturally he did not set up the soldiers the way a small child does, for the pleasure of knocking them over. He had at one time invented rather complicated manoeuvres for Lloyd Osbourne—war games which real officers at a military academy could have played with profit because it required a serious knowledge of tactics to execute them.

This was the war game Stevenson was playing, by himself and rather lonesomely in his step-grandson's nursery, on the evening of the day when he had come so close to a real war. The lead-soldier armies, on this occasion, represented the troops of Mataafa and Laupepa, and R. L. S., smoking an untold number of cigarettes, was working out a problem of strategy, with the aid of these seasoned and remarkably well-disciplined soldiers; it was the problem of an attack from the land side on Mulinuu, the seat of the Laupepa government. In this battle of Mulinuu, the righteous cause of Mataafa triumphed. It took a great deal of cunning to overcome the enemy's superiority, and the hardly won victory was celebrated by a triumphal entry of the victors into the capital city of Apia. A handsome lead soldier general headed the procession, and his brown horse really did look a lot like Stevenson's pony Jack.

122

CHAPTER VIII

THE BALL

ON the day after R. L. S. went almost to the camp of Mataafa and his rebels, when he almost put himself at the head of a revolutionary army to do great deeds of heroic valour, the monthly packet arrived in the roads of Apia. This was always a great occasion and naturally someone of the household had to ride into town to the post office. Usually the most powerful of the servants, Lafaele, went along with an immense linen sack to carry home the voluminous correspondence, letters, newspapers, and the mass of books which his writing colleagues throughout the world were in the habit of sending to R. L. S. The head of the house liked to ride in to meet the mail himself, but on this day he let Isobel go in his stead. (Did he, perhaps, fear that if he went to Apia again he might have another attack of heroics?)

The postmaster of Apia was an old grey-headed Englishman who was also the town photographer, and the room in his house which served as post office was cluttered with plates, frames and prints. While the postmaster and his fat Samoan housekeeper (an elderly lady who knew how to make the most of her exalted position) sorted the mail, the

123

inhabitants of Apia who were expecting letters either waited out on the open veranda or went into the post office itself and rummaged around in the mailbags. Consequently, everyone on the beach knew each letter that every other person received or dispatched. When Belle went into the post office on this particular day, she noticed that several people were looking with ill-concealed curiosity at the immense pile of mail sorted out for Vailima. Right on top lay a large envelope covered with impressive seals and an inscription which could be seen from a considerable distance: "On Her Majesty's Service."

Both the people who were still loitering around the post office and those who had come and gone were aware of the great news and carried it along the water front: Mr. Stevenson had received a letter from the Foreign Office, probably from the Foreign Secretary himself. The reason why this letter caused so much excitement was that for several days the whole beach had been making positive assertions to the effect that Stevenson was going to be deported as a troublemaker and that Her Britannic Majesty's High Commissioner for the South Seas would shortly communicate this to him. Moreover, the news shook the confidence of the rather numerous anti-Tusitala party, for it was hard to believe that Lord Rosebery would himself communicate with a person suspect and delinquent. Others insisted that yes, it was a deportation order, but that it was couched in considerate form because he was a celebrated man.

Belle herself was not quite sure what to think, and she was a little disturbed by the fateful-looking letter. For a brief moment she held it in her hand and struggled with the temptation to open it then and there. But when she saw the people standing around, craning their necks to watch her, she put the letter with the seals into her own pocket, while Lafaele stuffed the great mass of the mail into his linen sack.

When she reached Vailima, Belle rushed to her stepfather's study and handed the letter to him with a dramatic gesture. The whole family gathered around to hear the contents of the letter from the Foreign Office.

Inside the elaborate envelope there really was a message written in his own hand by the man who was guiding Britain's foreign policy. Lord Rosebery, in polite and friendly phrases, confessed to a passion for collecting autographs, and would Mr. Stevenson be so kind as to send him a fine signature for his album? Such was the real matter contained in the letter that all Apia was talking about at the moment.

Louis opened one letter after another and indicated briefly to his secretary Belle which ones were to be answered and in what manner; for on this one day his whole budget of mail for a month had to be cared for. The great majority of letters came from autograph seekers, although they were not all as illustrious as Lord Rosebery. If the request was put to Stevenson in proper form or at any rate in an appealing way, he usually granted it, and sent either a short sentence or verse, on a sheet of paper, duly signed. If the correspondent showed himself to be stupid or impertinent, or if he wrote Stevenson's name incorrectly (R. L. S. could not tolerate that), he fumed for a bit and then threw the annoying communication into the wastepaper basket. Yet one letter in today's batch, which was addressed to "Mr. Stephenson" was laid aside as a curiosity. It read:

"Dear Mr. Stephenson, I have read all of your works. I look upon you as the greatest living writer. Please send me a complete set of Samoa stamps."

Another quite unknown applicant asked for money—not much, only ten pounds—in return for which he offered to Mr. Stevenson, his favourite author, an angora goat, provided, of course, that he would pay for the transport of the animal to Samoa. Still another wanted money for a ticket to Samoa so that he could come out and help the missionaries; on the side he proposed to run a chicken farm.

There were a few kindly and pleasant letters in the collection. A few of Stevenson's readers succeeded in finding expressions of gratitude which did not smack too much of sheer flattery and self-importance. A little boy in England put in a violent and somewhat bold plea for a new book "exactly like *Treasure Island*." Others spoke of some poem which had pleased them, or else they alluded to Stevenson's new novel in a way which showed that they had read it with affection and understanding. To such correspondents, and especially to the little boy, R. L. S. sent immediate answers, dictated to

Isobel. He also wrote to authors who had sent him books for criticism; except when the book of a young beginner was too hopelessly bad. In such cases he preferred not to say anything.

His private correspondence, his letters to his personal friends, to his mother in Scotland, to Sidney Colvin and Charles Baxter, who looked out for his business affairs, were already partly written, but if letters from them had come in the mail, then these had to be completed or revised.

This routine of mail day, with the inevitable correspondence of a world famous author, was sometimes a burden to R. L. S., but not so this time. He had not recovered sufficiently from the excitement of yesterday to get down to work again. For all the vivid grip that *Weir of Hermiston* had had on him yesterday as he sat in Faamuina's house, today he had been able to get a word of it on paper. There was too much tension in the air for work, so he was very glad to have guests in for luncheon; they were no less than His Excellency the Catholic Bishop of Oceania and the French priest who accompanied him.

Although Stevenson came from a family of ardent Protestants, he liked to surround himself with Catholics, and the majority of his native servants were "popes," as they called them in Samoa. Consequently the Bishop's visit was a great occasion for the household of Tusitala. When His Excellency, followed by Father Rémy, entered the dining room, all three of the servants knelt before him and kissed his bishop's ring. The white-haired, white-bearded Bishop was dressed in white, with a lavender sash, and as he gave the boys his blessing Stevenson, with the eye of an artist, watched the scene, the picturesqueness of which was enhanced by the Scottish-Samoan costumes of his servants. Meanwhile the Bishop's secretary or chaplain, whichever he was, had made the acquaintance of the ladies of the house. He was a lively little fellow, not nearly so sedate as his Bishop, rather merry in a way peculiar to the French and not disinclined to some-what worldly jokes.

As the English of these two clerics was well-nigh unin-telligible, French was spoken during the meal. This was a language which R. L. S. spoke with great elegance, and Lloyd also knew well; Isobel and Graham had an Anglo-Saxon ac-cent, but Fanny did not include a talent for languages among the many she possessed. Over and over again, with her char-acteristic liveliness, she would make a sally into the conversa-tion only to get stuck, and flounder desperately in search of a word.

The discussion, which naturally turned around the subject of the impending civil war, eventually boiled down to a con-versation among the two priests and Stevenson. The Bishop and Father Rémy were, in their hearts, on the side of the good Catholic Mataafa, but they did not choose to give free rein to the expression of their sympathies, because there were some Catholics on the other side and the Mission was offi-cially neutral. Nor did the guests forget that they were in a Protestant household; neither the Bishop nor Father Rémy knew many Protestants at close range and they had a more or less incorrect idea of them. The jolly chaplain trotted out his usual stock of stories based on episodes in the Bible, as though they were brand new, and as though he were dealing with a table full of good, but completely ignorant, little children. R. L. S. had grown up in a Presbyterian atmosphere and knew the Bible by heart, so that he was able to note a number of little slips on the part of the lively priest; but, of course, he said nothing.

When Louis was a little boy, he had dreamed of becoming a minister in the Church of Scotland. He could hardly speak properly when he had already begun to put on some sort of robes and climb up on chairs and preach. Later on, the puritanical atmosphere of his parental home was bound to throw him into the arms of the atheists; the young bohemian in the black velvet jacket, who consorted with English and French artists in the Seventies, belonged to the cynics and the skeptics. But out here in Samoa, especially when his pious old mother was in the house, he gave evidence of a changed attitude toward religion. He conducted religious services for the natives in his household, and composed beautiful, if not too orthodox, prayers; sometimes, albeit rather seldom, he even accompanied his womenfolk into Apia to church, and kept up friendly relations with the missionaries of the various denominations which were active in Samoa.

Who can really tell what R. L. S. believed in his innermost heart? It was hardly possible that a man who was obliged to think about death a hundred times every day should be untouched by religious considerations. His brand of religion would undoubtedly, had he ever described it to His Excellency the Bishop of Oceania, have seemed to be the very worst kind of heresy. It so happened that toward the end of the very good meal (Talolo was an extraordinary cook and had, as a good Catholic, done his best for the Bishop), followed by the warming effects of Stevenson's old Madeira, the talk had come around to Father Damien, the martyr and apostle to the lepers in Hawaii. Stevenson had visited the leper colony on Molokai, he had known this dour but heroic priest and had come to admire him. When an overzealous missionary of his own Presbyterian church had dared to defame Damien's memory with some coarse expressions, he had come out in a fiery defense of him which was full of even more emphatic terms. R. L. S. spoke in similar language of the heroic Catholic nurses and nuns on Molokai. Judging from this, and from Tusitala's preference for the Catholic Mataafa, and also from his having a Catholic household, the Bishop might have been tempted to have hopes of converting this heretical worldling. Perhaps even his visit of today had something to do with these hopes, and also Père Rémy's pious Biblical anecdotes which he so casually recounted.

Yet somehow or other—perhaps it was due to the famous Madeira wine of the hospitable house of Vailima—the conversation on religious topics kept digressing in spite of all the efforts of the Bishop and the chaplain to keep to the point. So the Bishop, in a very dignified manner, blessed the servants again, took farewell of his hosts and rode off with his secretary.

After which, so the record reveals, Stevenson devoted what was left of the afternoon after the visit of the clerics to the frivolous occupation of having Belle teach him certain dance steps. He had an unrequited love of dancing, and for tomorrow, war or no war, he had accepted an invitation to a great ball in Apia.

All the balls in the Samoan capital took place in the "Public Hall," a barnlike building which served for gatherings of all descriptions. Stevenson, as a notable of the colony, was chairman of the managing committee of the Hall. Perhaps this was why he felt obliged to attend the ball with his family, although he was hardly in a mood for any such entertainment. In his earlier, gypsy existence, as a free and unencumbered artist, he would never have felt any such compulsion; but now as a public dignitary of the beach, chief of the clan of Tusitala and a political party, and besides as husband of Fanny and the stepfather of two such devotees of the dance as Lloyd and Isobel, he was distinctly under obligation to put in a dignified official appearance at the ball.

On this particular day, the Friday before the civil war in Samoa was to break loose in all seriousness, and before the "Public Hall" was to be converted into an improvised military hospital, Stevenson would have been glad to get out of going to a dance. By evening he was tired; he had given in to Isobel's insistence and ridden over again that afternoon to the place where he had seen Mataafa's outposts. But the sketches she had planned to make did not amount to much. This time there were no picturesque warriors at the ford; in fact, it almost looked as though, at the eleventh hour, Mataafa had abandoned his prospective revolt. On the other hand, the beach was alive with rumours about the plans of the opposite party, the Malietoas; they said that the King was now going to attack. In the bar of the "International," where R. L. S. and Belle stopped to drink a lemonade, one man told them quite definitely about the plan to make a surprise attack on Vailima and plunder it. This might have served as a sufficient reason for staying at home that evening and guarding the threatened premises. But Stevenson was determined to make a show of the fact that he did not believe the rumour and that in any case he was not afraid, so he decided to go to the ball. They sent their party clothes on ahead to the house of some friends, rode into town after supper and arrayed themselves in all their finery; the gentlemen wore the customary full dress of the tropics, which is to say, patent leather shoes, dress trousers, white jackets and gayly colored sashes. Isobel put on the obligatory white silk dress—only half-castes would go to a ball in coloured gowns—and Fanny, whose colouring was too dark to stand the stark contrast of white, dressed herself in the black velvet creation she had bought on her last trip to Sydney.

At the gate in front of the dance hall Stevenson suppressed a yawn; he was tired and did not feel any too well. Then he offered his arm to his wife, and the whole family made its formal entrance into the ballroom.

The Public Hall was decorated in the usual manner with flags, palms and paper garlands, and oil lamps contributed a none too brilliant illumination; to be quite frank, the great room, like all such places in the tropics, looked undeniably desolate. In spite of the unsettled times, or perhaps even on account of them, every last person who could lay any possible claim to being in society, and who was not a missionary and therefore automatically excluded from the sinful pleasure of the dance, put in an appearance. To be sure, the officers of the two German men-of-war now in the roads at Apia had not come, and that was a bad sign; the vessels must be in a state of preparedness for eventualities or else nothing could have kept the lieutenants or the midshipmen away from the ball. Otherwise, all of the socially available white upper crust of Apia were on hand: the clerks of the German Plantations Society and representatives of the other European enterprises, several independent traders, the captains of merchant ships now in the harbour, and even several doubtful people belonging to the beach, admitted on condition that they washed themselves and wore suits of clothes. There was not a single Samoan man to be seen, but there were several lovely Samoan women there, who were married to whites, and who had come with their half-blood daughters.

Fanua smiled from across the room to her friend Tusitala and showed her fine white teeth as she did so. Fanua was the daughter of the High Chief of the Apia region, and her official name was Mrs. Edwin Gurr; her husband was a New Zealander who had settled in Apia. He was a lawyer and attorney before the Supreme Court, and something of a banker besides; he handled Stevenson's affairs. The two men were on very friendly terms, but the great friendship between Tusitala and Fanua dated back before her wedding—at which Tusitala had danced—to the time when she was the official maid of honour, the Taupò of Apia. He had known her in the fantastic garb of her office and now she appeared, fully dressed in European style, at the ball. But otherwise she was the same old Fanua, an impulsive, warmhearted soul, who could never be civilized.

Now she ran across the ballroom as R. L. S. came in and kissed him without any trace of embarrassment before she had even greeted Fanny or the others in his party.

"Oh, Tusitala!" she called out as she ran over, "I am so glad you had the letter from Queen Victoria and are going to be allowed to stay here!"

The news about the letter with the inscription "On Her Majesty's Service" had spread through the whole town, and

Tusitala's standing had been freshly buttressed by it. Up to this point the clear assumption had been that Sir John Thurston, Her Majesty's High Commissioner in the Western South Seas, would act in the matter of the expulsion of this writer, who had made himself obnoxious through his newspaper articles and his promotion of Mataafa's cause. And now he was found to be in high favour among the reigning Olympians in London. As Stevenson crossed the ballroom, with Fanua in her bright red silk dress on his arm, people thronged around and spoke to him in the hope of gleaning some further details about the sensational letter he was supposed to have received. But he only smiled, diplomatically, and betrayed nothing; he was full of impish glee over the fact that an envelope under Lord Rosebery's private seal had sufficed to cause a fundamental change in his political standing. Even the British Consul General, who had shown a certain reserve of late towards the household of Vailima, radiated cordiality.

The official personages of Apia, the consuls, the Chief Justice, the President of the Municipality, the Land Commissioners, did not appear in the ballroom until the party was in full swing, but they arrived in time for the great quadrille, which was, of course, as always at the balls in Apia, led by Wurmbrand. Captain Wurmbrand was the name given him by the misinformed, and those who were not sure of their ground called him Baron; actually he was Count Robert von Wurmbrand-Stuppach, a retired captain of the Imperial and Royal Cavalry—and at present a beachcomber, or something

135

suspiciously like it. His brother was equerry to Franz Ferdinand, heir to the Austrian throne; he had himself played a distinguished part in the Bosnian campaign, and no one knew how he had become stranded out in the South Seas or what he was really doing there. He was a tall, broad-shouldered man, with a heavy, dark beard. He lived entirely alone in a tiny shack on the beach; he was always out of pocket and gladly undertook any kind of casual work. He was indebted to Robert Louis Stevenson for many a commission and friendly service. He was the embodiment of good humour and good nature. As he stood there in the ballroom, dressed in a perfectly cut dress suit, but with very old, cracked patent leather shoes, he looked like the aristocrat he really was, in spite of his wild-appearing tramp's beard.

As a dancing master he was incomparable. In contrast with a Court Ball in Vienna, this affair in the Public Hall of Apia undoubtedly left something to be desired, but that was not in any way the fault of the wonderful leader of the quadrille, who called the figures in the purest of French: "Chassez-croisez!"

R. L. S. danced the quadrille with Fanua. Whenever he came near her, he could smell the intoxicating perfume of the garlands of white flowers she had draped over her European ball gown.

The music consisted of a harmonium, an accordian and a fiddle. The man who played the fiddle was not Middy; he

136

had already left Samoa, shipping as a steward on some sailing vessel or off to some gold mining camp or other.

It was close in the hall. It smelled of perspiration, cheap perfumes, kerosene and also of the heavy scent of the frangipani blossoms outside in the garden.

Stevenson was an incurably bad dancer, but he threw himself into the quadrille with the greatest of ardour, as he did into anything he undertook, and he tried with a deadly earnestness to go through the steps just as he had practiced them at home with Fanny, Belle and Lloyd. At first he would be painfully careful about the position of his feet, but then his mind would wander, and occasionally he would throw a whole figure into confusion. There was a great deal of confusion in the dance anyway, in spite of all the efforts of Count von Wurmbrand. It took R. L. S. some time to find out who the gentleman opposite him might be, and when he did discover who it was, he was so taken aback he stopped dead in his tracks; it was the Chief Justice Cedercrantz!

Ever since this Swedish gentleman had assumed his office at the court of King Laupepa, he and Stevenson had cordially hated each other. In his letters to the *Times,* Stevenson had over and over again characterized Laupepa's European advisers as incapable mischief-makers; they had retorted by using their influence to have him expelled from Samoa on the grounds of his being a disturber of the peace and an opponent of the official policy of the Great Powers. At this moment, when the very thing had occurred about which

137

Stevenson had been warning them, the civil war in Samoa, the consensus of opinion was that the position of the German President of the Municipality, Senfft von Pilsach, had been considerably undermined. He had gone off on a suspiciously long leave of absence, and moreover it was thought, on good authority, that Cedercrantz was about to be recalled. Should this happen, it must necessarily be attributed to R. L. S. And here they were, at the very height of the crisis, these two men who had not even seen each other for some time, standing up, in the middle of the ballroom, as participants in a ridiculous quadrille; each one had a red sash around his middle, and it so happened that they were the only red sashes in the whole hall. As the dance figures brought them close to each other, they looked as though they belonged together, Robert Louis Stevenson and Conrad Cedercrantz. At their last previous meeting the Justice, in his official capacity, had shouted very angrily at Tusitala, who had not taken it kindly. And now here they were dancing away for all they were worth and both were smiling, while outside perhaps the first shot in the civil war was being fired.

The blond Swede's face was smiling, and it showed no sign of embarrassment as he danced toward his opponent. He was entirely absorbed in the intricacies of the quadrille, and perhaps it did not even occur to him then that the thin man opposite him in the figure had, with his biting articles, cost him his good position here in Samoa and brought everything down around his ears.

Stevenson watched him dance and said to himself: Do I really hate this man? Personally I am inclined to like him; he is really rather nice, and he cannot help having been sent here to fill an office for which he is unsuited.

He stopped short right in the middle of one of the most complicated figures and threw everyone out of step. The grotesqueness of his situation had suddenly been borne in on him. What was he doing here? What was it all about anyway? It was a silly parody of the ball on the eve of Waterloo, when the cannon were already beginning to roar.

When Fanua saw that her partner's absent-mindedness had completely wrecked the quadrille, she adroitly extricated him from the turmoil and led him to the buffet, where refreshments were being served by a Chinese restaurant keeper. Stevenson hastily quenched his thirst with a bowl of kava. He gently disengaged himself from Fanua and walked over to the door that led into the garden. He gave one glance back into the hall; Fanny was dancing with Graham. She would have scolded had she seen him going out into the open all heated from dancing. But outside the night was warm, and all the stars of the South Seas shone in the heavens. Outside one could hear the pounding of the surf as it crashed along the cliffs. Or could that be the sound of shots from over towards Malie?

CHAPTER IX

BLOODY HEADS

THE civil war in Samoa, which everyone had foreseen and no one had prevented, least of all the so-called Protecting Powers of the tiny Island kingdom, broke out during the second week of July. It was not a real war at all as Europeans understand the meaning of the word. Many of the battles developed out of kava banquets, where representatives of both sides were present, and they were also the result of the endless speeches, the wild war dances and weird ceremonies which accompanied the festivals. When it came to the point of real fighting, neither side allowed itself to display any undignified excess of eagerness, as the Papalangi would surely have done. If some palisaded fortress was being besieged, the attackers, after a hot and strenuous day of fighting, went home to have a good night's sleep in their villages, leaving the besieged in peace. Next morning the warriors returned to their positions, each duly accompanied by his wife who carried his weapons and his lunch. The warrior himself carried only an umbrella, for the weather in Samoa is very uncertain.

But, of course, there were some peaceful and beautiful

villages destroyed and people were wounded and even killed. And the real purpose, after all, of a war in Samoa is to cut off the heads of the dead and the wounded in order to display them as trophies of victory. The Samoans, in fact, found it particularly difficult to understand why the whites who lived out in their islands, and especially the missionaries, were so opposed to this warlike practice, and showed so much more aversion and horror over it than they did over the actual killing. The Samoans were only playing the manly game of war according to their own national rules.

Immediately after the first engagements, the fortunes of war turned decidedly against Mataafa, whom King Laupepa branded as a rebel, and in whom Tusitala saw the one capable statesman among all the chieftains of Samoa. Apparently he had overestimated his influence. The majority of Samoans remained on the side of the more or less legitimate government, or remained neutral out of fear of the guns of the foreign men-of-war. Mataafa's men were attacked by the royal troops, uniformed in their red kerchiefs, near the village of Vaitele; a lot of gunpowder was set off, and the loyalists bagged a dozen heads and carried them back in triumph to Mulinuu, to Laupepa's official residence, while the defeated Mataafists withdrew behind the bulwarks of Malie.

There was a special reason for rejoicing at the victory feast in Mulinuu, because among the captured heads one was found to have belonged to a son or a nephew of Mataafa (the Samoans have the same word for the two degrees of

141

parentage so that it was impossible to establish which he really was). The old Frog King sat in state on the veranda of his European-style house, and the victorious warriors laid the captured heads at his feet with much singing, dancing and yelling. This was done according to old Samoan traditions, which were probably a last remaining vestige of a state of cannibalism long since rooted out in this part of the South Seas. The custom was that whoever had slain a man with his own hand carried the head to the king, holding it by the hair with his teeth. In the course of these savage entertainments, a little incident occurred which was to have a great influence on the further history of Laupepa and his Island kingdom. As the heads of the enemy victims were brought and spat out on the ground before the king, it was noticed that one among them was that of a woman. More than that, it was the head of the "Taupò" of the Island of Savaii, a highly honoured, sacred virgin of the high nobility, whose duty it was to preside over all the village rites, dances and kava ceremonies, as well as to represent her clan on all occasions. When war had broken out, this vestal had transformed herself into a kind of Amazon. Her long hair, which used to be plaited with shells, feathers, and bits of mirror, had been cut off to make a warlike headdress for her father, the High Chief of his clan. Then she had dutifully carried her father's arms as he went into battle. That was a general custom; during the fighting the Samoan women carried water and munitions to their husbands and fathers right into the

142

line of battle. One of these Amazons might accidentally get shot, although no Samoan fighter, even in the hottest kind of contest, would dream of consciously hurting a woman or a child when a village was seized. And to cut off the head of a woman who had fallen in battle was even more unheard of. That this should have happened, unless it was because an inattentive warrior in the excitement of victory had mistaken the shorn head of the Taupò for a man's head, would go to prove that under the influence of white civilization, Samoan customs had become distinctly more savage. However that may be, the old King Laupepa was painfully ashamed when he saw the woman's head among the pile of trophies. He ordered it immediately to be wrapped in the most costly piece of silk which his palace had to offer. A herald then carried it to Malie, to Mataafa, and was commissioned to make a great speech of apology. Nevertheless, Samoans of all parties threw the blame for the incident on old Laupepa personally, and this was one of the things which later enabled another rival, Tamasese, to arise and overturn his weak government, carrying down to final defeat the native control of Samoa.

As for Mataafa, he was blockaded by Laupepa's partisans immediately after the battle at Vaitele. But the King's men were neither unified nor energetic in their behaviour, so that he succeeded in broad daylight in launching his war canoes and leaving Malie after he had fired the village. After he left the island of Upolu, he landed in Savaii, the other most important island in the Samoa Archipelago. He expected to find a number of loyal followers there. But since the tide of luck in war had turned against him, one section of the chiefs of Savaii declared against him; another maintained a doubtful neutrality and called for a "Fono," a parliament of High Chiefs. There they would drink kava, and after lengthy speeches by the official Talking Men the question of the royal succession would be settled. Mataafa did not think the prospects promising and realized that he would not be able to assert himself in Savaii; he decided to try his luck on still another island, on Manono, whose villages and fertile coco plantations were now exposed to fire and pillage.

At this moment, barely one week after the commencement of hostilities, when Mataafa was settling the remnant of his army on Manono, Her Britannic Majesty's man-of-war, *Katoomba*, arrived in the roads of Apia. If the British Admiralty had sent this Captain Blickford and his ship a little more promptly, Mataafa's rebellion might very well not have occurred, for Blickford brought with him definite orders to support Laupepa with armed force. That was just what the commanders of the two German battleships lying in the harbour of Apia had been waiting for; until they were sure of Great Britain's position they were not willing to proceed against Mataafa, in spite of his recent unpopularity with the Germans. Now the three men-of-war, the two German and the one British, steamed off together to Manono, and they threatened Mataafa with bombardment and the landing of marines unless he agreed to surrender himself. Faced with

144

such overwhelming odds, he naturally had no choice but to capitulate. Accompanied by a small group of his most distinguished supporters, among whom was the old chieftain Faamuina, Mataafa was taken on board one of the German ships and transported to the Marshall Islands. On the very same island of Jaluit where once upon a time Laupepa had lived in exile as a prisoner of Bismarck, Mataafa, his cousin and enemy, was now destined to spend many unhappy days.

This marked neither the end of Mataafa's political career nor yet the final triumph of Laupepa. As things developed later, the favour of the German colonial policy was eventually to turn away from Laupepa and to restore Mataafa to a kind of power. But for the present his case seemed to be hopeless; his supporters were hounded on all sides. Confiscation of their property and arrests were the order of the day. A number of chieftains and commoners were put into a primitive prison camp not far from Apia. In happier times many of them had enjoyed the hospitality of the house of Vailima. Nor did Tusitala abandon them in their dark days.

During the actual hostilities the Stevenson family had never been seriously molested. There was never the slightest hint that the wild rumours of an attack on Vailima might be substantiated. R. L. S. had had some dream of defending his home with his gun in his hand, but now he did not know whether to be glad or sorry when he found how completely he was left in peace.

145

He had gone through the first few days of the civil war in a daze. He rode into Apia to see the war canoes of the King's party which were gathered there. Each one was supplied with a drummer and a bugler, in addition to a champion fighter and an exhibition war dancer. This last was like the man he had seen in front of Faamuina's house. He stood in the nose of the canoe and cut all kinds of inciting capers, while the drummer rolled his drum, and the bugler maltreated his European instrument by blowing painfully false notes on it, in addition to all of which the fighters, from time to time, let out menacing war whoops. This savage war fleet lay in the harbour of Apia, and for a day or two the town was swarming with black faces and red bandanas; then the King's men left, moving westward to the accompaniment of warlike din. A little later the first wounded began to pour into Apia. The news of this reached Vailima in the evening after dinner. Whereupon Stevenson, Lloyd and Fanny ordered horses and lanterns and rode through the cold starlit night into the town, to the mission where the wounded were being temporarily cared for. Stevenson was in a state of suppressed excitement. The first sight which met his eyes when he reached the mission was that of a badly wounded man who had been shot through the lungs. He lay there dying, surrounded by a group of wailing relatives. As soon as he saw blood spurting out of another man's lungs, Stevenson became both calm and energetic. He placed himself at the disposal of the bespectacled Miss Large, who was assigned to organize

146

the care of the wounded. A larger place was needed, so R. L. S. went out in the middle of the night to wake the committee and obtain permission to use the Public Hall. One idiotic member of the committee raised some objection, and the ensuing midnight debate left R. L. S. excited and worked up. When he had finally convinced him, he went back to the mission and found that the surgeons from the two German war vessels and their aides were at work operating. For the first time in his life, which had been full of illness and the contemplation of death, R. L. S. saw human beings dying. Uli, the chief, whose lung had been pierced by a bullet, was a beautiful young man. He lay there, mercifully dazed by narcotics, and groaned faintly, as his friends stood by his bed and stroked his feet. Stevenson stretched out his hand and touched him lightly. It made a strange chill run through him; it almost seemed to him that he saw himself lying there, with death in his lung.

In the grey light of dawn the Stevensons rode home; they had not yet heard the result of the battle in Vaitele. But when R. L. S. went to Apia the next day to help Miss Large establish the new hospital in the Public Hall, he had the news of Mataafa's defeat, of King Laupepa's victory feast and of the Taupò's head. There was another gruesome story current about a head; one of the triumphant warriors had washed the head of his victim before presenting it to the King. When the gore was wiped away, and the face of the dead man was revealed, what should he prove to be but the

147

warrior's own brother! That is the real countenance of civil war, thought R. L. S.

He took refuge from his powerlessness and his despair in his work. In a letter to his friend, Sidney Colvin, he quoted Candide's saying: *"Il faut cultiver son jardin"*—that old, hopeful yet resigned formula of men of letters who cannot take any active part in world affairs. While the flames of war were flaring to the sky, Stevenson's literary garden flourished. His story of adventure, *St. Ives,* made notable progress. He carefully rewrote once more all the beginning of his great novel, *Weir of Hermiston.* And since the mail packet was leaving—on the very day when the fighting was at its height—he sent off his literary correspondence with his usual punctuality; so many letters to publishers, to admirers, to autograph collectors. There was even a letter to Henry James, containing an estimate of a sonnet by José Maria de Heredia. Another was addressed to Conan Doyle, whose most recent book, Stevenson said, had unfortunately not yet arrived, but he was awaiting it with eagerness. He also wrote to a distant cousin, James S. Stevenson, to clear up an obscure point in their family genealogy; for in addition to the adventures of St. Ives and the story of the house of Weir of Hermiston, during these days of Samoan civil war distress, R. L. S. was writing the biography of his grandfather, who had built lighthouses on the coast of Scotland.

"Il faut cultiver son jardin."

So the summer passed. Besides the war, there were private troubles to be reckoned with. Belle had an attack of malaria. Then Lloyd and Graham came down with dysentery. "Belly belong him" was the name given to that unpleasant illness by the black boys on the plantation. Then Stevenson himself, for a change, took to his bed. It was only a slight hemorrhage, a reminder and a warning. The beautiful youth, the Samoan fighter whom R. L. S. had seen in the hospital, was not the only one whose lungs bled. One can die on other battlefields than fighting before a palisade, spear and club in hand.

By September it almost seemed as if there had been no war. Which is to say that as long as the foreign battleships lay in the vicinity of Samoa, there was peace within the shadow of their guns. The household of Vailima was on the most cordial terms with the officers and men of the British cruiser *Katoomba,* the very ship which precipitated Mataafa's downfall, for Stevenson was first of all a British patriot. One fine September day the proprietor of Vailima, with the consent of the captain of the vessel, invited the whole ship's band to a party. The bluejackets marched out to Vailima to the tune of their own fifes, drums and bugles, while all the children of the town and villages gathered along the way to gape at them. The House of the Five Rivers was decorated with flags, ferns and garlands of heavily scented flowers. As soon as the white hats of the sailors were visible, Simele, as major-domo, went down to the gate to

149

greet them. In addition to his loincloth, he wore a white shirt and a black coat so that he really looked like the butler of some fine English establishment. This made a profound impression on the bluejackets. They halted for a moment at the gate; then the drummer gave a mighty roll and the ship's band boomed its way into the estate of Vailima. On the lawn in front of the house they finished their piece. The clearing was filled with Samoans who had gathered to see them. Among them were many lovely girls, dressed in, rather than adorned by, flowers, and they smiled sweetly on the sailors. There was nothing to remind them of war and desolation, or of the lost freedom of Samoa.

Inside the house these hardy seamen found two huge tables laden with the most luscious fruits, and also with ham sandwiches, cold chicken, cakes and coffee. There were three immense containers filled with lemonade which had been laced with rum and claret; and beer also flowed freely. The British tars ate and drank until they were red and blue in the face. In between courses they went out onto the veranda and gave performances on their brass instruments which shook the house. Later, when their mood had been somewhat mellowed by the influence of alcohol, they staged a lyrical concert by one of their members who played the guitar and accompanied himself as he sang a sentimental ditty about a poor beggar who stood endlessly and in vain in front of the house of a certain Jasper, and begged for a crust of bread. Then the garlanded sirens took their turn, singing their dance songs, sitting and swaying their arms and their voluptuous bosoms to the rhythm. After which the Samoan men, also flower-bedecked, gave a magnificent savage war dance. Some of them had recently been in the real war on Mataafa's side, now Tusitala had given them work on his plantation so that they could earn the heavy war fine which the victorious government had levied on them. But now they were concerned with contributing to the best of their abilities to the entertainment of the sailors from the *Katoomba*, who had really been the cause of their defeat.

In other words, it was a successful party, gay and patriotic, and it filled the hearts of both the Samoans and the British with equal enthusiasm.

During the time of the crisis, Robert Louis Stevenson had comforted himself in a manner consonant with being an exemplary patriot, a substantial paterfamilias and a notable citizen. But on the very day after the party for the sailors from the *Katoomba* he suddenly left Samoa; he ran away from this burden of his respectability.

His excuse was the need of a rest. Graham Balfour, his tall cousin, wanted to go to Hawaii, to undertake from there a long cruise among the islands. Without giving his household any warning at all, Stevenson abruptly announced that he was going to accompany his cousin as far as Honolulu, and spend several weeks there. Fanny had noticed the storm signals in her husband's increased nervousness and the frequent and groundless outbreaks of temper that had occurred lately, and she had the good sense to say that she would not go along. She understood her husband extremely well; if she let him run himself tired, he would come back to Vailima soon enough.

Perhaps Lloyd had some qualms about whether or not he should offer to go with his stepfather on his journey. But he said nothing. They decided that Talolo would go to Honolulu to take care of Tusitala. Of all the servants in the house, he was the one who spoke the best English, and he was passionately devoted to his master. For the Samoan youth to go on a sea journey by steamship was a tremendous thing, if for no other reason than that it necessitated his wearing trousers for the first time in his life, over his tattooed legs. He felt himself to be completely disguised and unrecognizable as he went to say good-bye to his wife in his Papalangi dress and then went on board the steamer *Mariposa* with Tusitala and Palema.

CHAPTER X

THE SILVER THISTLE

THIS was not Robert Louis Stevenson's first visit to the Hawaiian Islands. During his great cruise through the South Seas he had stopped there for six months with his mother, Fanny and Lloyd, to take a rest or rather to get some work done. That was in 1889. At that time Isobel and her husband, the American painter Joe Strong, were living in Honolulu. Joe enjoyed a position equivalent to that of a court painter to his brown Majesty King David Kalakaua, who was still the independent ruler of the Archipelago, and Isobel was a teacher of drawing on the faculty of the Royal High School. She was in such high favour with the clever, alcoholic, poker-playing South Seas monarch that he had bestowed on her the insignia of the Order of Oceania, which she had previously designed. Consequently, when the Stevensons arrived, they naturally stepped right into the splendour of court life and were soon looked upon as partisans of the King, in contrast to the other white residents in Honolulu, who were classed as belonging to the Mission Party (which was as much as to say that they were in favour of the annexation of Hawaii by the United States, of the rapid importation of Asiatic coolies for the sugar plantations, and were generally on the side of Business). Like all romanticists, Stevenson was a born and lifelong royalist. He would have sided with the House of Kamehameha the Great in any case, even if he had not already grown so fond of the Polynesians and sponsored the political independence of their little Island kingdoms on cultural grounds. This did not mean that he had found his dreamed-of ideal of a king in fat, bewhiskered Kalakaua, who aped European ways, gave large Court Balls and in his private life left a trail of empty champagne bottles. What had happened was that while he was living near the beach at Waikiki, and working on his *Master of Ballantrae,* Stevenson had met the most adorable little Princess who could ever enthrall a Scotsman already enamoured of the South Seas. Moreover, she was a kind of countrywoman of his because her father was a Scot, with a goatee, by the name of Cleyhorn, who had married an Hawaiian Princess, the younger sister of King Kalakaua. Since the King had no sons, his half-Scottish niece, the little Princess Kaiulani, might in certain circumstances have succeeded to the throne. What a stroke of luck for an enthusiastic legitimist like Robert Louis Stevenson to have this charming little Scottish-Kanaka member of one of the oldest princely families in Polynesia as a subject for his lyric adoration! She lived with her father at Waikiki, not far from where R. L. S. had rented a house. He went over frequently to call on Governor Cleyhorn. He would sit out in the court beside the Princess and talk to her in a fatherly tone, albeit with the deference due from a loyal subject. She might have been a daughter of the Stuarts and he a Scottish cavalier, who had pledged his sword to her and sworn to be faithful unto death. When she was sent to England, nay, to Scotland, to get the advantages of a European education, the Scottish poet wrote some lovely verses to her in her album and added these lines: "written in April to Kaiulani in the April of her age; and at Waikiki, within easy walk of Kaiulani's banyan! When she comes to my land and her father's, and the rain beats upon the window (as I fear it will), let her look at this page, it shall be like a weed gathered and pressed at home; and she will remember her own islands, and the shadow of the mighty tree; and she will hear the peacocks screaming in the dusk and the wind blowing in the palms; and she will think of her father, sitting there alone."

The tactful writer did not add of whom else the little Princess should think, but what he meant was clear.

At that time it would not have taken much to persuade R. L. S. to settle in Hawaii instead of going on to Samoa. But perhaps he did not like it so well after the little Princess left Honolulu; the town, he declared, looked much too civilized to him. It was a half-baked city well on the way to acquiring a European lack of distinction, and to live through this period could not be a pleasure to any good European. Not long after Kaiulani set out for Scotland, the Stevensons left to pursue their journey.

As they were leaving, after they had taken their farewells from their friends in Honolulu, and just as their vessel, the *Equator,* was weighing anchor, King Kalakaua came aboard to bid them good-bye. He brought his Court Band along, together with a number of bottles of champagne which he proceeded to consume in his own right royal person.

Now when R. L. S. came back to Hawaii after three and a half eventful years, he found everything changed. The good King Kalakaua had drunk himself into his grave, and his sister, Queen Liliuokalani, who had succeeded him on the throne, reigned only for two years; then she had been deposed by the mission party. Now she was leading a lonely existence in her palace on Beretania Street, and Hawaii was being run by a Provisional Government commonly referred to as the P. G. This P. G. meant just one thing: the preparation for annexation by the United States and the end of the last independent native kingdom in Polynesia.

Yet in those earlier days Stevenson had sat on the Lanai of the Royal Palace beside the last descendant of Kamehameha, that Napoleon of the South Seas, beside the fat, good-natured, bewhiskered King Kalakaua; and sitting there with fragrant garlands around their necks, they had talked together of a dream of a greater federation of all the island kingdoms where the Polynesian tongue is spoken. In addition to Hawaii, that would have included Tahiti, Samoa, Tonga and all the tiny islets with their native kings whom R. L. S.

had visited on his cruise through the region of the Thousand Islands, and with whom he had pledged brotherhood. Kalakaua had thought seriously enough of the project to send an embassy to Samoa to further the plan. Perhaps, too, the poet R. L. S. had dreamed another dream: of a coral throne in an Empire of the South Seas. But, of course, he would not have set good old Kalakaua on it. No, it would have been offered to the youth of Polynesia, whose charm would have been embodied in the lovely Kaiulani. And perhaps, standing on the top step near the throne, there might have stood a fatherly, devoted and loyal figure, that of a slim Scottish bard, with the Star of Oceania over his faithful heart. . . .

If he ever had had those dreams, they were all at an end now. In Hawaii, as in Samoa and Tahiti, the colonial interests of the great foreign powers had triumphed over the romance of the islands.

These half-ridiculous, half-touching Kanaka kingdoms were fading away before they could effectively assimilate the modern civilization which was destroying them. And yet the people of Hawaii, Samoa and Tahiti had been happy under their island kings; they had covered themselves with flowers and laughed all day long.

Immediately on his arrival, Stevenson called on the deposed Queen Liliuokalani in her palace. He had known her in the days of her glory, and she reminded him wistfully of the great banquet in Hawaiian style which he had held in his house in honour of her and her brother Kalakaua. Those were the days! And the Queen began to weep. Stevenson was not the person to recall to an unhappy woman that she had perhaps not been the wisest of rulers, and that during her short reign she had committed one folly after another. He tried to comfort her; but he knew that in no circumstances would she ever sit on the throne again. The Royalist Party, which was then conducting a desperate last-ditch campaign, had the intention of giving the crown of Kamehameha, not to Liliuokalani, but to her niece Kaiulani.

O poor Kaiulani! At that very moment the little Scottish Princess of the South Seas was in Stevenson's own city of Edinburgh, and she was having the same difficulty which he used to have; she could not stand the climate. Like Stevenson, she too was well on the way to dying of sick lungs, while her loyal cavalier sat under the banyan tree at her father's house and spun royal dreams for her. Perhaps, while they were talking together, these two Scots really did believe in the romantic possibility of making the sweet little Kaiulani Queen. But when Stevenson broached the subject with others, the Kanakas shrugged their shoulders resignedly, and the whites politely covered up their smiles.

The white population of Hawaii, the missionaries, planters and traders looked upon R. L. S. as a great writer, but in politics they thought him somewhat crazy, for they all knew about his disastrous espousal of Mataafa's cause, and they now expected him to make some dramatic gesture on behalf of the fallen dynasty of Kamehameha, to stage some romantic act, or at least write some provocative letters to the *Times*. Yet none of all this occurred. Stevenson did not so much as mention politics. Whenever any curious or tactless person began to gloat over the deposed dynasty or abuse the ex-Queen in his presence, he either held his tongue or used his great skill in conversation to lead the discussion in some other direction. In an interview, he told the editor of the English newspaper published in Honolulu that he was a friend of the Polynesians and a royalist, that he hoped, in spite of the mistakes she had made, the United States would put the Queen back on her throne. But when the editor began to lecture him, on the basis of many years of experience, to the effect that the Polynesians were incapable of handling their own interests, Stevenson immediately switched to the topic of his own literary plans, to the great South Seas novel he wanted to write, in which he would paint the whole picture of that world of islands with the white missionaries, traders, planters, beachcombers and, of course, the Polynesians—for you know, he added, with a light shrug of the shoulders, they really do exist in the world!

Perhaps, as he talked to his interviewer, he had in mind what Sir George Grey had hoped: that he, Robert Louis Stevenson, might prove to be the great instrument of destiny which would preserve the Kanakas of Polynesia from being completely wiped off the face of the earth.

After the departure of Graham Balfour in his sailboat, R. L. S. and his faithful servant Talolo lived in an hotel on the beach at Waikiki. It bore the pretentious name of "Sans Souci-by-the-Sea," but was for all that a rather simple boardinghouse. Out here, several miles from the city, he hoped to have some quiet. But he was now a much more famous man than he had been on his first visit to Honolulu. Not only did copy-hungry reporters beat a trail to his door, but English and American tourists as well found their way to Sans Souci, hoping to see, to speak to, or even to touch this celebrity. Stevenson was nearly always accessible to reporters, even when they came so early that he was still in bed, or not feeling well; but the stupid curiosity of the celebrity-stalkers often grated on his nerves and at times he could be most unpleasant. This was the experience of one English tourist who was overaffable with R. L. S. and not affable enough to Talolo.

Hawaii was a country of marvels for that young Samoan who had never set foot out of his homeland before, and Honolulu was an entrancing fairy-tale city. There was nothing in Apia to which he could even compare the unbelievable things he saw in Honolulu. Perhaps in London, the famous city of Queen Victoria, things were done with the same High Chief magnificence, but that was hardly credible. For days he

160

was fascinated by the donkey-drawn tramway which took them into town from Waikiki; but when he saw the real railway which carried passengers to Pearl Harbour, he was speechless. Everything which the Papalangi—they were called Haoles here although they were the same people—did in Hawaii was imposing and bewildering, quite different from Apia. But then the Kanakas were different too. When the brown people of Hawaii talked among themselves, the Samoan often understood what they were saying, but there were times when he could not make it out at all. His own name, for instance, was pronounced so strangely: Kalolo. On the other hand they laughed when he spoke of the great old King who had ruled over them as Tamehameha. The two Polynesian dialects were so different, in spite of their similarities, that Talolo was often tempted to try English in his efforts to get the Hawaiians to understand what he was saying. But there he ran into the difficulty that even English was pronounced differently in Hawaii from the way it was spoken in Samoa. How could Talolo guess that "keonimanu" stood for gentleman and that "kuna" was the equivalent of schooner? As a consequence of these linguistic difficulties, especially the cursed substitution of *k,* which he somehow could not master, Talolo had a hard time finding his way around in the perplexing traffic of a big city. Besides, Tusitala took a puckish glee in sending the boy on complicated errands, with a long list of addresses on a slip of paper. Talolo was obliged to inquire his way around, and when he came back home

Tusitala had him describe his odyssey and his little adventures in every detail, and sometimes he laughed so hard it shook every joint in his thin body. Talolo's comments on things Hawaiian were a source of delight to R. L. S. and teasing and testing him day after day, he grew more and more fond of the young Samoan. Nevertheless, in his excitement over the marvels of Honolulu, Talolo never forgot that he had been sent along to care for Tusitala and to serve him, and he even bore in mind that his real position was that of cook in the house of Vailima. So he haunted the hotel kitchens and Chinese cookshops in town to discover tempting new recipes he would try out later at home. He also watched the Hawaiians prepare their national dishes. In short, he was an extremely busy and happy young man and he was prepared, should the necessity arise, to go through fire and flame for Tusitala.

One morning both master and servant had errands to do in town. As usual, Stevenson sent Talolo on ahead, and he went off to call on some acquaintances. They were to meet again at noon in the Hawaiian Hotel. They met at the door and went in together; Tusitala laid his hand lightly on Talolo's shoulder and together they walked through the billiard room to the bar. It was a hot day and it called for a cold drink, perhaps some coconut milk with a little gin or Stevenson's special lemonade, for they had been walking in the streets for a long time. The billiard room was full of people Stevenson knew, or who recognized him, and a chatty group gathered around him; Talolo stepped modestly aside. An English tourist, to whom the celebrity had been pointed out, joined the crowd without being invited, and said, "Have a drink?" Yes, a cool drink was just what they all did want, so Stevenson accepted the stranger's proffered invitation in the name of his friends, beckoned to Talolo and said with a smile: "This is my friend Talolo; he is thirsty too." The Englishman was deeply shocked that he should be asked to take a drink with a coloured man. He looked dazed for a moment and then said to the bartender: "Very well, give the boy a drink—over there." And he indicated a far corner of the bar, some distance away from where R. L. S. and his acquaintances were standing.

Robert Louis Stevenson was offended to the depths of his heart, but he maintained an icy calm. He said: "I do not know your name, Sir, but it seems that Talolo is not good enough to drink with you. I fear, Sir, that neither am I. Come, Talolo, let us go to the dining room. I am hungry."

That the world-famous author treated his Samoan "boy" as though he were his son was no secret to the other boarders at Sans Souci; nor did any other detail of his external life escape their sharp eyes. They knew that he arose late in the morning (what did these boarders know of his morning's work in bed!), that he walked restlessly up and down in the garden, or strolled out to the end of the pier, where he would sit motionless, with fixed gaze, in the fierce sun, watching the fantastically coloured sea. They observed, too, that he ate little as he sat alone at his table, and that he would sit for hours over a glass of California claret, looking absent-mindedly at a design on the wall of the dining room, which Joe and Isobel Strong had painted during their stay in Honolulu. They noticed that on some days Stevenson spoke to no one except Talolo, but that on others he had an almost frantic craving for company and made numerous calls on friends in town or visited old Cleyhorn, the father of Princess Kaiulani. It even happened occasionally that he would be sociable and chatty with the other boarders. He would gather them around him, of a hot afternoon, out on the lawn under the umbrella-shaped trees. Anyone who passed might have heard Stevenson's voice speaking, followed by an explosion of laughter on the part of his audience. When he set himself to be witty and entertaining, he carried everyone with him.

At other times, towards sunset, he often sat alone on the veranda, with his eternal cigarette in his hand, watching the light fade behind the purple mountains of Wainae.

How alone and desperate he felt during all this time was something that his chance acquaintances had not noticed. They also failed to understand why, on one fine evening and apparently without any reason, he lost his head. He overheard two gentlemen at a neighbouring table discussing an article by the well-known journalist, Wickham Steed, which had been published in the *Review of Reviews*. The effect on Stevenson of the very mention of the name of Wickham

Steed was like waving a red rag to a bull; he banged his fist on his table with such violence that his claret sprayed the cloth and he began to pour out a flood of derogatory remarks about him. What he had to say was not very coherent, but it was clear that he had been enraged by some remarks of Steed's about a member of the Royal Family in a recently published article. This outburst of rage was brief but terrifying. R. L. S. glared at one table after another to see if anyone would dare say a good word for Steed or show any expression of disloyalty to the British Royal Family. But as everyone present only stared back at him in embarrassed silence, he gulped down the few remaining drops of wine in his glass, and rushed angrily out of the room.

A little later he went to the proprietor and shyly apologized for his behaviour.

A few days after this unaccountably strange scene, the guests in the Hotel Sans Souci noticed that both for luncheon and for dinner the table of their illustrious fellow boarder was unoccupied. They heard that he had had a bad hemorrhage and was lying in his room, ill. Talolo was stopped in the hotel corridors and subjected to sympathetic inquiries every time he came out of Stevenson's room. Stories were current of the self-sacrificing care with which the youth surrounded his sick master; at night he slept on the floor by his bed. Nevertheless, he was not the most experienced nurse, so Dr. Trousseau, the French doctor in charge of the famous patient, felt it necessary to send word to Mrs. Stevenson in Samoa of her husband's state of health and to ask her to come as soon as possible to Honolulu. She started by the very next boat.

Whatever had caused Louis to leave home so suddenly, and whatever was the nature of the spiritual crisis through which he had been passing in those weeks in Honolulu, now that he was so weak, he was extremely happy to have Fanny by his sickbed, to have her take his physical care together with his whole being into her brown hands. Theirs was one of those happy marriages from which there was no escape.

After Fanny had nursed him back to life, he began to behave once more as a famous author and a happy pater-familias, which was to say he behaved himself normally and decorously.

He sat to the sculptor Hutchinson, who did a bust of him, and who made also a plaster cast of his right hand, the hand which had written *Treasure Island*.

He attended an official luncheon, given in his honour, on board the American man-of-war lying in the harbour; and in spite of the fact that on this occasion a member of the Provisional Government made the most tactless possible remarks about the Hawaiian Royal Family and the Kanakas in general, R. L. S. did not throw his wine glass in his face, but maintained a dignified and discreet silence.

Also he gave a lecture at the Scottish Thistle Club.

166

In Honolulu, as everywhere where Anglo-Saxons live, there was a special Scottish colony which did not mix either with the English or the Americans. These Scots of Hawaii met at their club, on occasion, to celebrate the birthday of some national hero, Robert Burns, Walter Scott or Robert Louis Stevenson, and sometimes they just came together to smoke, drink some Scotch whiskey and chat in their own dialect. Stevenson's picture had hung from the beginning next to those of the other great Scots on the walls of the Club; and now that the writer was himself in Honolulu, the Thistle Club decided to bestow on him the high rank of "honorary chieftain." The deputation which bore the news to the man thus honoured also extended an invitation to him to come to the Club and make an address. Fanny did not feel that the convalescent's state of health warranted the acceptance of the invitation and she raised some objections, but Stevenson was stubborn about it and insisted on giving the lecture. On the Thursday before the Stevensons and Talolo were to leave Honolulu, there was an oppressively large crowd at the Thistle Club. The rooms were beautifully decorated with flags, ferns and crosses of St. Andrew; they had even raked up a few nearly authentic thistles.

Stevenson arrived on the scene, accompanied by Fanny. He still looked ill and was wrapped in all sorts of capes, shawls and mufflers, as a protection against the cold night air, on his way to the club. He stepped up onto the platform and made a witty address, in the course of which he reviewed

167

the whole history of Scotland. It was, however, far from being a fulsome, patriotic account; in fact, when he had finished, Scotland did not have a leg left to stand on. He said he could not imagine why it was that they were all so inordinately proud of being Scots; but they were. R. L. S. was apparently unwilling to give his whole approval to any of their famous heroes, not to William Wallace, Robert Bruce, or even to Mary, Queen of Scots; although he did admit to a weakness for this beautiful and hapless lady. He did not show any real warmth for his subject, as he went rapidly through the past of his fatherland, until he came to the Rising of 1745 and began to tell of the romantic escape of Bonny Prince Charlie. He even allowed himself to hark back to his own novels, in which he had glowingly described the places and the personalities connected with the famous flight. He said: "With Prince Charlie Scottish history comes to an end"—but he did not by any means bring his own speech to a conclusion at that point. Somehow or other he managed to get around to the Lord Chief Justice of Scotland, formerly known as the "Hanging Judge." This jurist was long since dead and had no real relation to the discourse, but he was the prototype of the main figure in the novel, *Weir of Hermiston,* on which Stevenson was working, with the consequence that the thoughts of the writer put words into the mouth of the orator.

Then he told one more good Scottish joke and ended his talk on a melancholy and slightly sentimental note: "Now,

168

when I think of my latter end, as I do less frequently as it seems more imminent, I feel that when I shall come to die out here among these beautiful islands, I shall have lost something that has been my due—my native, predestined and forfeited grave among the honest Scotch sods . . . on one of our purple hills under one of our old, quaint and half-obliterated table-tombstones slanting down the brae. . . ."

The Scots of Honolulu were much touched, and applauded while Robert Louis Stevenson smiled for a little before he bowed his thanks. But on that brief moment he saw his grave open before him, not a grave on a purple heather-clad mountain in Scotland, but on the top of Mt. Vaea.

The all-pervading feeling of sentimentality in the hall called for some expression, so they all joined hands and sang "Auld Lang Syne."

Before R. L. S. left Honolulu, the president of the Scottish Club gave him their emblem, a little silver thistle, to wear in his buttonhole. A surge of warm feeling went through him and he said: "I shall always wear it."

And he did; it was always fastened in the buttonhole of his brown velvet jacket, over his Scottish heart.

The last person to bid him farewell on the ship was Cleyhorn, father of the little Princess who to him was the symbol of the two countries he loved, Scotland and Polynesia. Cleyhorn said with foreboding:

169

"Kaiulani has written at last. But she is ill, she has a heavy cold. I hope it is nothing serious. . . ."

"Oh, yes, I know; it is our climate back home in Scotland," replied Stevenson with a sigh. He took one last look at the breath-takingly beautiful outline of the harbour of Honolulu, with the smoking volcano and the blue mountain chain in the distance. Then he shook hands cordially with Kaiulani's Scottish father, and went below with Fanny.

CHAPTER XI

PRISONERS OF WAR

IT was in the early days of November that Stevenson returned to Vailima, to his books and manuscripts, to the almost princely magnificence of his semibarbaric household, to social intercourse with his white and native friends, to great Samoan banquets, where the guests used their fingers to eat pigs roasted in the ground, and to dinner parties where evening dress was obligatory. He went back to all that, but not to Samoan politics. Which did not mean that he would neglect for a moment his duty as a good friend to Mataafa and his partisans, who were now down on their luck.

On his faraway island of exile, in Jaluit, Mataafa was the recipient of substantial proofs of Tusitala's faithful remembrance. Every ship that went from Samoa to Jaluit carried presents to the prisoner King and his loyal comrades; materials for shirts and loincloths, great sacks of kava roots and all of the things that Tusitala knew would warm the heart of a Samoan. And if he was so thoughtful of the exiles, he did much more for Mataafa's followers and companions who had remained behind in Samoa.

The chieftains who had been most deeply implicated on

Mataafa's side in the civil war were put into a prison camp, which was situated in the mangrove swamps between Apia and Laupepa's royal residence in Mulinuu. The prison, which was not suitable for housing a large number of people, consisted of one small, gloomy building and was surrounded by a far from imposing enclosure of corrugated iron. There were just a few dark cells. When the Austrian Count von Wurmbrand, that jack-of-all-trades, was named to the high position of commandant of this state prison of the Kingdom of Samoa, he immediately ordered the construction in the prison yard of a number of huts in the native style. After that the High Chiefs, who had been crowded into six tiny cells, led a much pleasanter life. The few attendants who had followed their masters into captivity never spoke of these huts in the prison yard except by the designation in High Chief dialect which means palace.

Wurmbrand had undertaken this gaoler job, which was a rather unusual one for a former officer of the Imperial and Royal Cavalry, because it would give him a regular salary, and that was a most welcome item to him just then. But King Malietoa Laupepa's so-called government had less money than ever after the civil war, so that the prison commandant's income was for the most part nonexistent; moreover, the kindhearted Count had to share the little he did receive with his prisoners, or they would have starved to death. For a while, in fact, during the time that R. L. S. was in Hawaii, they suffered severely from privation. Then the

Count had had a life-saving inspiration: he allowed his prisoners of state to receive their feudal followers who had remained outside the prison, and these brought in so much food of every kind that not only were the prisoners well fed but also the heavily bearded face of Count Robert von Wurmbrand-Stuppach grew fatter and broader. Even the royal guard, which had been detailed to mount watch over the prison, had a share in the abundant supply of delicious food. In short, the friendliest of relations existed between the guarded and their guards; and they all shared in a common affection for Tusitala, who, as soon as he returned, became the patron saint of this jovial prison, the provider of unlimited tobacco, of never-ending kava. He was the rich man of Samoa, whose bottle imp produced whatever he asked for and he generously shared his abundance with his friends.

About Christmas the flow of provisions increased to such an extent that the warden of the prison and his inmates sent a joint invitation to a great banquet in the prison to Tusitala and his family.

Stevenson had really had his fill of banquets. Only a few days previously they had celebrated—a little late—his own birthday, or, as they had jokingly announced, the birthday of Miss Anne Ide. She was one of the three lovely daughters of the new Chief Justice of Samoa, and she had had the bad luck to be born on Christmas Day, so she never had a real birthday party of her own or any real birthday presents.

173

R. L. S. liked this young American girl and felt so sorry for her plight that one day he formally made over his own birthday, the thirteenth of November, to her. This was done by means of an imposing document, all signed and sealed and presented with appropriate speeches. After that, in Vailima, she was no longer known as Anne, but was called Louise in honour of the great Louis; and when the birthday came round each year, they all pretended that it was Louise and not Louis who was the centre of the celebration; all the congratulatory messages and presents were for the young girl, and the master of the house shared in a part of them only out of a feeling of sympathy for him because he had no birthday at all any more.

Immediately after this remarkable double birthday party, sixteen guests were invited to Vailima to celebrate Christmas Eve. This was a memorable occasion for the natives, for they saw in Tusitala's house a magic and unheard-of thing, something they had never seen before—a Christmas tree. On Christmas Day the whole family was exhausted and would have liked to put in most of the day sleeping; but there could naturally be no question of their breaking their promise to go to the gala dinner at the prison. So all the Stevenson family, aching and groaning, got up at half-past two in the afternoon, drank some tea and dressed themselves. Lloyd was of the party. Sosimo and two of the "boys" had been sent on ahead to take some presents to the prisoners, a live pig and a basket of pineapples.

It was an excruciatingly hot day for Christmas; one realized how complete the contrast was at the Antipodes to the glorious cold climate back home. The sweating horses had to be urged on to cover the four and a half miles to the prison camp. The last bit was particularly hard going; they had to cross a dangerous turf causeway which led them through horrible snaky mangrove roots over a foul-smelling bog.

A crowd had gathered at the gate of the prison to see Tusitala. Two sentries, at either side of the entrance, presented arms and let the foreigners in without any question; in fact it looked as though anyone could go in and out of that gateway.

Inside the corrugated iron wall was an open place which glowed with reflected heat. At first glance it looked like a market place. All around, on the ground, were piles and pyramids of foodstuffs of every kind, sort and description; pigs were tethered to stakes, and huge turtles lay helpless on their backs, kicking in the air. The first impression was of the gargantuan abundance of the food supply, and then of the excellent smell which came from the direction of the cooking pits. Then came the intermittent sound of the Talking Man's voice, announcing in loud and impressive tones the list of rich High Chief gifts that had been sent to the prisoners. Stevenson, who certainly had nothing with which to reproach himself when it came to the giving of gifts (he possessed none of the characteristic parsimony jokingly or seriously attributed to the Scots), suddenly was over-

175

whelmed with the painful regret that he had brought so little along. He had been actuated by a sense of delicacy because today he was to appear as the guest and not the benefactor of the prisoners; but when the silly herald began to enumerate each little pineapple Tusitala had sent, and with such pomposity, R. L. S. wished he might have made a better entry in the general gift-giving competition.

Here the whole group of prisoner chieftains arrived to greet him. They were magnificently attired in Samoan fashion, each with an "ula" around his neck, a chain made of scarlet seeds from some rare bush. The highest in rank among them was also the tallest, for in Samoa a "High Chief" really is, in nearly every instance, an outstanding figure. This one was called Auilua and was a handsome warrior type. R. L. S. told Lloyd that he made him think of Homer's Ajax. "Why especially Ajax?" asked Lloyd Osbourne, laughingly. "I don't know," said R. L. S., "but it is not of Achilles or Patroclus he reminds me, but Ajax, son of Telamon."

Then Count von Wurmbrand, stroking his dark beard, stepped forward to welcome the guests. When the exchange of greetings was over they all, guests, prisoners and warden, dropped down on all fours and crawled through the low entrance to one of the "palaces" which had been erected in the yard, and where a great and elaborate kava ceremony had been prepared. They squatted in a semicircle; the chieftain Auilua presided and made a sign to Fanny to sit on a mat at his right; they were planning, so Auilua explained, to

176

drink kava today "in true English fashion," as it might be done at the court of the legendary Queen Victoria. For that reason a number of lovely Samoan maidens had been placed on the opposite side of the hut from the guests, on the freshly swept floor. They were dressed in short skirts of grass and rushes, and were otherwise naked except for the necklaces of shells and garlands of fragrant flowers they had around their necks. They prepared the kava according to the English style, which was to say they refrained from chewing the root and spitting it into the wooden bowl; today they grated the kava roots, watered the pulpy mass and pressed it through a sieve of palm fibres. Thus they paid due respect both to the barbaric custom of their faraway island, and to the childish prejudices of the Papalangi. That the "taupò" does not chew and spit the kava out in London before she presents it to the guests of honour was something they rather prided themselves on knowing in Samoa.

Even the ceremonial presentation of the kava was executed according to the best information about the etiquette prescribed by the court of Queen Victoria. The unheard-of novelty was introduced of serving the ladies first. The dignitary who was acting as "kava caller" made a complimentary presentation speech in Fanny's honour, and then he came to the point of ordering the coconut bowl taken to the Mistress Aolele; but instead of calling her by that name, he outdid himself and proclaimed: "To the Miss Seteveni." Isobel's name was pronounced in an equally perfect English rendering; it sounded something like Strao. But when Tusitala's turn came to take the first ceremonial sip of kava, he abandoned the prevailing tone of Anglomania; he loudly and clearly announced the libation in Samoan to the old heathen gods of the island—an important part of an official kava drinking. Then he reached out his hand, in which he held the cup, somewhat behind him and poured out a few drops as he said:

"Ia taumafa e le atua. Ua mantangofie le fesila-faga nei."

"Be it partaken of by the God. How beautiful to view is this High Chief gathering."

Then he clapped his hands three times and drank the opaque liquid.

R. L. S. made an extraordinarily successful impression with this solemnly intoned heathen prayer. After him every one of the chieftains as he was called to partake of the kava repeated the ancient saying: "Be it partaken of by the God!" Then turning to Tusitala, with an earnest and affectionate look, he raised his cup to him and said: "Soi fua! Long may you live!"

Every time that wish was expressed a pang, at the same time painful and comforting, went through Tusitala.

After the kava-drinking rituals had been carried out, they all moved to another hut and again they squatted, in true English style, on the ground, at places laid with green leaves. Before they began to eat, Auilua made a sign at which each chieftain took off his beautiful "ula," his long and valuable

178

necklace of rare scarlet seeds, and laid it around the neck of one of the guests. The latter were politely reluctant to accept any such valuable present; it was an honour altogether too great. But Auilua—who reminded R. L. S. of Ajax—insisted that they accept the necklaces and that they be sure to wear them as they rode home past the palace of Malietoa Laupepa. It seems that the old King had sent word to the chieftains that he was having a feast the next day and that they were all to send him in their ulas. But this they were loath to do; they said they would much prefer to give them to Tusitala.

Nor was this all. After the banquet they again returned to the hut where they had drunk the kava, and lo and behold! in the meantime a whole Christmas celebration had been prepared for Tusitala and his family. All the beautiful presents which were piled up there had been made by the womenfolk and the followers of the prisoner chieftains; they had not bought anything, said Auilua, for they had no money, they were living in slavery; but for Tusitala, their one friend in time of trouble, they still had presents. He enumerated each gift separately, and as he did so he added in a voice full of triumph: "This is a present from the poor prisoners to the rich man, Tusitala!" There were thirteen lengths of "tapa," a shimmering material covered with lovely designs, which the Polynesian women make out of the fibres of certain trees and then dye in the most beautiful colours. Then there were thirty fans, each of a different colour and shape, a particularly handsomely polished kava bowl and a number of delicately wrought tortoise-shell rings. All the while that the High Chief was making his half-pathetic, half-humorous speech inside the hut, a herald was standing out in the yard, and his voice was distinctly audible as he told off the list of foodstuffs which were also destined for Tusitala and his High Chief palace; the amount was overpowering, colossal, staggering. Stevenson had brought along three "boys," but he said that they would never be able to carry off so many wonderful things; that they had better leave the presents there and send for them the next day. But that would never do. It seems that the presents were to be carried in triumph through Mulinuu, past the King's residence. "Make 'em jella" was the expression used by the interpreter in his funny beach-English.

Just before the end of the entertainment something of an inexplicable nature happened. A party of people suddenly rushed into the prison yard, past the ever-passive sentries. There was an uproar and everyone jabbering at everyone else in Samoan, of which the Stevensons could not understand a single word. Auilua, the chief, who had just been smiling so amiably, jumped from his seat with a roar; and now Stevenson realized why he had made him think of the raging Ajax. R. L. S. half-feared and half-hoped that some dangerous happening was in the offing; perhaps the partisans of Tamasese were raiding the prison; perhaps they intended to capture Tusitala and his family as hostages and drag them off to the interior of the island, to the mountains where this

third pretender to the Samoan throne had established himself, out of reach of the guns of the foreign battleships. Or
was it only the usual rush that happens at the end of Samoan
banquets when the guests grab what is left over from the
feast?

In any case Count von Wurmbrand did not seem to have a
very clear notion of just what was going on, for he put on a
worried expression and was firm in ushering his visitors out
of the gate. "Do hurry, and get away as fast as you can!"

The two sentries presented arms. The gifts were laden, as
best they could be, on to the horses—five slaughtered hogs,
masses of breadfruit and taro, fish and turtles, tropical fruits
and bales of tapa. R. L. S. and his family felt a little grotesque
as the principal figures in this procession of heroic proportions, laden with sacrificial offerings, each one covered with
innumerable garlands of flowers and draped with bright red
ulas. Young Lloyd Osbourne rode at the head, and at one
point he turned around and called back, with one of his rare
boyish laughs: "Thank goodness, I have at last had the wish
of my life fulfilled: I am riding in a circus parade!"

The "circus parade" started off over the turf causeway and
reached Mulinuu. It went past the residence of King Laupepa (he did not appear so they could not say whether it
"make 'em jella") ; then they filed past the headquarters of
the German Plantation Society into Apia, and then along the
whole length of the beach. Everywhere their route was lined
with an admiring public which exclaimed: "Manaia!"—"Oh,

how beautiful!" Even Lloyd Osbourne's glasses flashed; his
eyes were shining with pleasure.

Yes, it was a great triumph for Tusitala, and the prisoner
chieftains of the Mataafa party had certainly had a good slap
at the King!

Not long after this occasion the wheel of Samoan politics,
steered by invisible hands, changed its course completely.
Without any obvious reason, Mataafa's followers were freed
from captivity. That was all very well for them, but what
about poor Count von Wurmbrand, who was now out of a
job as prison warden? He went to see his friend Stevenson
and told him his troubles; whereupon R. L. S. realized something which had never occurred to him before—that on his
Vailima plantation they were very much in need of a super-
overseer, a kind of gentleman cowboy, to look out for their
cattle; and who could fit the situation better than an ex-
cavalryman?

So it happened that during the daytime one might see the
Count, with a broad-brimmed hat on his head, riding out
behind the cows. And of an evening, by lamplight, he was
to be found in the great hall teaching the household to dance,
with all the decorum which his brother, equerry to the Arch-
duke-Heir Presumptive, might exhibit at a Court Ball. Consequently, no one regretted that the prisoners had been set free,
not even their gaoler.

CHAPTER XII

THE NASSAU DREAM

THAT charming old adventurer, Count von Wurmbrand, was a friend—certainly one for evenings when nothing was going on at Vailima. But there were many other friends to be found in Samoa; Fanua's husband, Edwin Gurr, was one of them, and the same might be said of Anne Ide's father, the new Chief Justice, and this or that missionary. In fact, the term would include most of the white residents of Apia with the exception of a few with whom Stevenson did not see eye to eye on political matters. Besides, among the natives, he had many manly yet childlike friends of whom he was fond and who loved him. In addition to the clansmen of his own household, and Mataafa's partisans, he loved and was beloved by people like Seumanutafa, chieftain of Apia— he was Fanua's father—and many others, whatever their vowel-laden names might be.

But Robert Louis Stevenson was homesick for the friends of his youth, for the men who did not know him as Tusitala, a plantation owner in Samoa, the honorary chieftain of the Tusitala clan, but who understood the artist, the bohemian, the intellect, which was in him. He longed for Sidney Colvin,

Charles Baxter, and above all for that friend of his youth whom he had loved and who had become estranged from him, William Ernest Henley.

When Tusitala thought of home, he thought of these three who meant home to him. For it is not true; one cannot long for purple heather-covered mountains as one can long for human beings.

R. L. S. thought of Henley as though he were dead. To be sure, they still exchanged an occasional book, a formal letter such as might pass between the poet Robert Louis Stevenson and the poet W. E. Henley. But a chasm had opened between them, one of those volcanic gulfs such as often suddenly yawns between two people of related artistic temperament, and no one knew the why and the wherefore of it all. Their friendship had dated from the day when the frail youth R. L. S. made his first visit, in the Edinburgh Infirmary, to the desperately ill W. E. H., and that friendship had blossomed as friendships can only in the springtime of youth. They had stuck together through trouble and play. They had been friendly rivals when together they wrote a number of tolerably good plays in Bournemouth, wasting a great deal of energy on this since neither of them was a playwright. . . .

Then something happened. It was a literary incident such as alienates writers from each other. It had to do with a story which Fanny attempted to write and which Henley claimed was a case of plagiarism, although not of his own

184

work. Fundamentally, the estrangement was based on a friend's dislike of his friend's wife; and vice versa. They quarrelled bitterly, became reconciled superficially, but were friends no longer. . . .

But that was past. His thought of Henley as dead soon changed to thoughts of his own death. It seemed to him as though that part of himself was already dead and buried. How could he sit down and write to his lost friend and say: Come to me; I am so lonely?

He wrote often to Sidney Colvin. In countless letters he implored this friend of his youth to come to visit him, to come at least as far as Honolulu to spend a few weeks with him, to the edge of his prison yard where he was held a hostage, not to laws but to climate.

"Colvin, you have to come here and see us in our native, mortal spot. I just don't seem to be able to make up my mind to your not coming. By this time, you will have seen Graham, I hope, and he will be able to tell you something about us, and something reliable. I shall feel for the first time as if you knew a little about Samoa after that. . . ."

That was what he had implored him to do in words, and between the lines.

Sidney Colvin, Professor and Keeper of Prints and Drawings in the British Museum, was a good, trusted and loyal friend. He was one of the sour kind of friends who, like tart apples, are often of the best variety. R. L. S. could rest assured that the manuscripts which he sent to him to London would be subjected to ruthless criticism. The whole world might praise the books of R. L. S., but Sidney Colvin would give them short shrift, although he and Charles Baxter together attended to their publication with care and affection. And, whenever he thought it pedagogically advisable, which was quite often, he would send severe and even bitter letters to Samoa. To this man in exile he owed at once friendship and an incorruptible duty as mentor. He could not be bribed by anything, not even by sympathy for the poor devil in his loneliness.

Every day when he walked through the colonnade in the British Museum, past the rigid idols from Easter Island, holding their mysterious watch, he should have been aware of the pleading call that was echoing across the South Seas to him. But perhaps the professor did not hear it, or he was terrified of seasickness, or his leave was not long enough, or he had to spend it elsewhere. . . .

None of the friends R. L. S. urged to visit him ever came. Others arrived, but they never came. And yet they were the ones who stood for youth, freedom, life.

Of course Stevenson was not really alone. He had Fanny, he had Belle and he had Lloyd.

But Fanny and Belle were women. It is an immutable law that friendship cannot exist between a man and a woman; it must be something more than that. More and not the same.

> "Trusty, dusky, vivid, true,
>   With eyes of gold and bramble-dew"—

That was how R. L. S. had described Fanny in his poem about her.

>   "Steel-true and blade-straight,
>   The great artificer
>   Made my mate.

> "Honour, anger, valour, fire;
>   A love that life could never tire,
>   Death quench or evil stir,
>   The mighty master
>   Gave to her.

> "Teacher, tender, comrade, wife,
>   A fellow-farer true through life,
>   Heart-whole and soul-free,
>   The august father
>   Gave to me."

Yes, but He did not give her to him to be a friend.

Lloyd Osbourne was different, too. He was a man and an artist; he seemed destined to be the friend after whom his stepfather yearned.

But he was his stepson.

This unreal relation of father to son was what stood between them, and it contributed more to keep the two men apart than the difference in their ages, more than the fame of the older writer which overshadowed that of the younger and often left him out in the cold.

After writing *Ebb Tide* together, their collaboration had ceased. The book was already in type when Colvin suddenly received a letter from R. L. S. in which he said that he wanted to have Lloyd Osbourne's name taken off the title page because the book was so bad he ought not to allow the young writer to be compromised by being connected with it. The letter arrived too late; the book appeared under the joint authorship of stepfather and stepson, and when the printed copies of it reached Samoa, R. L. S. was filled with a kind of paternal tenderness, for he had had no idea that it could have turned out nearly so well. Both the critical and material success of *Ebb Tide* rejoiced R. L. S.'s heart. But he never wrote another book with Lloyd.

Ever since R. L. S. had come back from Honolulu, Lloyd had fallen prey to a great restlessness. As soon as the war scare was more or less over, he could not stand it in Vailima any longer. In April, which is a winter month in the Antipodes, he suddenly remembered that snow and ice as in Davos were to be found within comparatively easy reach, in New Zealand. One could go skating on the Alpine lakes of the land of the Maoris!

So Lloyd Osbourne went off for a few weeks to New Zealand, to see the snow and ice, sleighs and skates once more. He said that he was homesick for all those familiar things.

188

It never really pierced his consciousness that what he really wanted was to see Davos again, where he had been the proprietor of the "Davos Press," where amid the ice and snow, he and Lou had both engaged in the fraternal enterprise of publishing books, two boys playing together on an equal footing.

He went to New Zealand and stayed away a long time.

In addition to Lloyd Osbourne, there was one other man with whom R. L. S. could talk freely on any subject, including literature.

This was an American by the name of Moors, H. J. Moors, a trader in South Seas produce. When the Stevensons first came to Samoa, after their cruises through the South Seas, they stayed with Moors. It was through the agency of Mr. Moors that they bought the piece of virgin bush land at the foot of Mt. Vaea, which they later transformed into their tropical estate of Vailima. Moors was a source of shrewd and sound advice to Stevenson in all business matters, and as there was no bank on the island, he took care of all money transactions. He had even sold him his beloved brown horse Jack, from his own stables. Before long Stevenson made use of his good friend's knowledge of Samoan background and conditions in another, less material way; when he wrote his little book, *A Foot-note to History,* describing the development of the political complications of Samoa, Moors' memories and stories were his chief source of information,

189

and the greater part of the book was written under Moors' roof. Moors was a great admirer of Mataafa, and it was through him that R. L. S. came to know and appreciate the pretender to the Samoan throne.

Even after the plantation at Vailima was fully established, Moors remained Stevenson's adviser. He, who knew the answers to all the problems of tropical agriculture, could look on with grim irony as the famous author and his diminutive wife carried out their amateurish schemes to make Vailima a productive enterprise. He was critical of Fanny's energetic but quite undirected efforts, as she planted cacao saplings with her own hands, and of R. L. S.'s feeble attempts at work in his own garden. Lloyd Osbourne's youthful attitude of superiority seemed like downright arrogance to Moors, and he certainly could not approve of turning the cattle raising in Vailima over to the Count cowboy; he advised much more rational methods than all that in their farming efforts.

Between Moors on the one hand, and Fanny and her children on the other, there was not much love lost; otherwise the relation between him and R. L. S. might have grown into one of those strong and steadying friendships between men of which Stevenson stood so badly in need and without which he was wilting away. In Moors he had found a critic who was sometimes ruthless and unjust, but always incorruptible and honest. In a world which was steadily more and more convinced of the greatness of this famous writer, there was only one other such person, Sidney Colvin, and he was sitting far away in the British Museum, looking at Japanese wood-cuts, and only occasionally dropping a gruff and friendly letter to Stevenson. Moors was not so learned as Professor Colvin, but he was just as hard on his prominent friend, and at least he was near by, within reach in Samoa.

But alas, he had not been at hand during those critical weeks when both Samoa's and Tusitala's destinies were being decided. During that particular summer of 1893, Mataafa's and Stevenson's ally had to go to Chicago on business. The World's Fair was going on there, and while Samoa was falling to pieces thousands of tourists in Chicago were daily admiring the Samoan Pavilion—the customs, manners and craftsmanship of the Samoans. Moors had instituted this exhibit and remained in Chicago throughout the Fair. When he came back, the old Samoa which he had been demonstrating with such affection to gaping visitors was gone—gone together with Mataafa.

The first meeting between Moors and Stevenson, after the former's return, took place at a luncheon party at the Hotel Tivoli, in an atmosphere of exaggerated gayety and alcoholic stimulation. The two friends wanted to have a quiet chat together, so after the meal, while the others went on drinking, Moors made a sign to Stevenson. They left together unobtrusively and climbed up the wooden staircase through the centre of the hotel to a tower. Up there they sat on a platform which commanded a beautiful outlook over the town, the harbour and the open sea. Stevenson wanted to plunge right into a discussion of Mataafa and the latest political developments in Samoa. But Moors said, in a severe tone, that he had read his last book, *Ebb Tide,* while in Chicago.

"'Well?" replied R. L. S., and hunched his long narrow head between his shoulders. He had a nervous premonition of what was in store for him.

"Not up to your level, Stevenson," said Moors severely. "Like all the rest of the books that you have written in combination with someone else, it is not up to your own level. *The Dynamiter,* on which your wife collaborated, was your worst novel; your plays have never been any good because you wrote them with some co-author, and now you are writing more books with this young man. Heavens, man, do use your head! Think, which are your best books, the ones which will last? *Treasure Island, Kidnapped, The Master of Ballantrae, Dr. Jekyll and Mr. Hyde.* Those are all books into which no one else put his fingers."

Stevenson's head sank deeper than ever between his shoulders; he felt as guilty as a little boy who is afraid of a spanking. The reference to the plays which he had written with his former friend Henley, stung him like the lash of a whip.

He snuffed out his tenth cigarette with his fingers and squirmed uneasily on his chair.

"I am writing by myself now," he said, as though to excuse himself. "I am working on two novels at the same time, *St. Ives* and *Weir of Hermiston.* But you know, old man, what

192

you say it is not all true! Do you realize that I shall make a great deal more money out of *Ebb Tide* than out of the *Master of Ballantrae* which you admire so much? The serial rights alone—"

"I am not talking about money," was the trader's curt reply. Whereupon Stevenson grew quite red in the face.

"It's no use talking, Moors," he went on. "Have you any idea what the running of Vailima and the big household costs me? Sometimes I think it would be better to give up writing entirely. One gets so weary of it, Moors. If I gave more of my time to the plantation, it would bring in better returns. Others prosper as planters out here in Samoa. . . ."

He gave Moors a sidelong glance, and saw a contemptuous smile on his lips. Suddenly, without any warning, Stevenson exploded. Overwhelmed by one of his furious attacks of rage, he jumped up, pushing his chair back so hard that it cracked.

"Don't sit there and grin like that, Moors! Damn you! Why don't you help me if you know so much better how to do things? How can I write even one decent line in this cursed place, in Vailima?"

He threw himself backwards with violence and then suddenly was silent. The man who sat opposite him and looked at his excited face with curiosity was not intimate enough with him for Stevenson to speak frankly about Fanny's restlessness and dominating love, of his complicated relation to Lloyd, and about the fact that he would long since have given

193

up writing his novel about St. Ives, for which he had lost all interest, were it not for the fact that his strict secretary Isobel kept spurring him on to finish it, whereas he would rather have worked on *Weir of Hermiston.*

He could breathe no word of all this, but before his eyes there arose that daydream which his hungry imagination one day had suggested to him. It was about a far place, quite, quite lonely . . . a South Seas island . . . but much more beautiful than this one, where there was no civilization, no politics, no . . .

("No death," was what a voice inside him said, but he brushed it aside and pretended not to hear its luring call.)

Off there, on his wonderful dream island, he would sit down on a beach, and give the best that was in him to his greatest work. . . .

Suddenly he turned to Moors with a slightly forced laugh.

"Well, when are we starting for the island of Nassau?" he asked abruptly.

Nassau was a tiny island five hundred miles to the east of the Samoa Archipelago. Stevenson had stopped there on his journey to Raratonga, and he had often raved to his friend Moors about the unspoiled beauty of the place. It really was still a paradise, untouched by the civilization which had ruined Hawaii, Tahiti, and now Samoa. It really was the South Sea island of his dreams! That is where he wanted to live, he had often said, and each time Moors had replied: "Let's do it, Stevenson, old man!"

And now, as he looked into his famous friend's face and heard him say it over again so slowly, he knew that this time Stevenson was in earnest.

"Hold on," Moors said: "I have a great surprise for you. On my way back from America, I stopped off at Nassau. It is really every bit as beautiful as you say it is. And just think, old Captain Ellacott, to whom the island belonged, has died, and I bought the place—lock, stock and barrel—from his widow. I have set a number of natives to work to put the property in a little better order, to clean up the house, the veranda, and the garden which had grown quite wild. Only say the word, old man, and you can go there, and no living soul will bother you while you write. . . ."

He stopped. R. L. S. had long since dropped back into his chair and was breathing heavily, in silence. Out on the sea a light breeze ruffled the sparkling surface of the water. Out there, somewhere in the invisible distance, lay the island of Nassau. There one could wander naked among the coco palms, or wear only the native loincloth. That would probably be the very thing for a man with sick lungs. Yes, that is how he could grow well again, in the warm, salty breeze. One could live there until one had really achieved something worth while. At least this one more book. . . .

With an abrupt change of thought Stevenson came back to the beginning of their conversation.

"You are quite right, Moors; my books up to this point have little value! They are nice stories for boys in their teens. None of them will outlive me. . . ."

"In any case *Dr. Jekyll and Mr. Hyde* will," was Moors' instant and sharp retort. R. L. S. made a grimace. That fantastic book on man's double nature had made him famous and wealthy, yet he had never liked it. Perhaps it was because it pictured the eternal struggle between the angel and demon that was forever being fought out in the depths of his own nature.

He said: "Oh that! . . . Well, you may depend on *Weir of Hermiston* being ever so much better than that. But not *St. Ives. St. Ives* is trash. Let's go to Nassau, Moors, so that I can finish *Weir of Hermiston* in peace!"

Sometimes a single word, or a thoughtlessly spoken phrase can change a destiny. Perhaps Stevenson might have followed in the steps of that other artist in the South Seas, Gauguin, and left his family. He might have ended his days in a native shack somewhere, if at that particular moment Moors had not begun to speak in a rather inimical way of Fanny.

"And what about your wife? And Mrs. Strong? How do you expect to get rid of the ladies for a while, my dear man? If I know Mistress Fanny. . ."

"Oh, I shall manage somehow," said R. L. S. but without any real conviction.

He went on talking idly of the plan, but already he had

lost his faith in the possibility of carrying it out; it was no longer anything but one of his charming conversational soap bubbles.

"You and I shall live alone together, Moors, like Robinson Crusoe and Friday. I shall do a lot of writing and you will, too. You will write down some of the lovely stories of the islands which you have been telling me."

"I am no writer," said Moors, who secretly had aspirations in that direction. He had written a number of articles for newspapers about the political and economic problems in the Pacific, and he rather prided himself on them.

"I'll help you with them," said R. L. S. encouragingly. "And you must help me too, of course. . . ."

Now I have involved myself so deeply, was the terrifying thought that flashed through Stevenson's mind, that if I had said one more word I should have asked him to collaborate on a novel with me, perhaps even *Weir of Hermiston.* I am capable of doing any foolish thing. I am so weak, I am always ready to lean on the first person I meet. Why, he is almost ready to be pleased about it! If anyone, I'd rather have Lloyd. . . .

He leaned back in his chair and once more the vision of Nassau passed before his eyes; the vision of a dream island in the South Seas . . . where more transparent waves were ever breaking in a more melodious way on a more beautiful coral reef. Even the brown natives were handsomer, gayer, singing under the coco palms, and there was never a mosquito. In one way Fanny seemed to be in the picture, and yet in other ways she was not there. He had fled from her and her domination, her importunate care, her cacao plants, her meals which she herself cooked, the perfumes she distilled, her terrifying homemade remedies which she obliged him to take, her violence, her moods. . . . On the other hand, part of her was there on the dream beach of the dream island—her warmth and her love. But this was not the usual Fanny, his wife. She was quite different. In this dream she bore the features of all the women Stevenson had loved up to that day in Grez, when he stepped through the hotel window and saw a charming, diminutive American lady, a Mrs. Osbourne. . . .

All at once it became clear to Robert Louis Stevenson that this was all a foolish dream. He had already run away to the South Seas to escape death, and he could run no farther. He knew that there was no dream island for him in the South Seas, and that what he really was longing for was his youth. Yet he let Moors talk on about the details of his plan, whose real but unavowed purpose was to get his jealously loved friend away for a while where he could have him to himself. He painted to R. L. S., who listened attentively and politely, the idyllic and yet comfortable life they would live on Nassau —without any womenfolk too. Stevenson even put in a few remarks which might have indicated that he was seriously thinking of going through with the project, and might be ready, perhaps sometime in the future, to go away with

Moors to Nassau. But the proposal which Moors was expecting, that he, the possessor of such a remarkable knowledge of the South Seas and the author of such excellent articles on that subject, should collaborate with the talented writer to produce a book—not the kind of stuff he had been weak and irresponsible enough to allow other collaborators to foist on him, but a really good book—that proposal was not forthcoming. So it happened that Moors, who had pressing business which took him back to the United States, and Stevenson never met again. Nothing ever came of Robert Louis Stevenson's attempt to make one more flight, to find one more refuge, or of his wild and desperate dream about the island of Nassau.

CHAPTER XIII

WHO MADE GOD?

IT was a Sunday evening in Vailima. The big conch shell, whose original function had been to call the members of a tribe to war, was now blown to summon the household and the plantation workers to prayers. Tusitala, the members of his family, and a few guests were already seated at one end of the dimly lighted hall. Now the handsome brown natives came in, men, women and children, for the most part clad only in their lava-lava loincloths, but well rubbed with oil and wreathed in holiday fashion with fresh leaves and flowers. Some of them brought lanterns, which they set on the floor beside them as they squatted in a semicircle. The hanging chandelier gave some light, but not enough to dispell the deep shadows in the great hall. In the semidarkness the gold statues of Buddha placed on either side of the staircase gave off a mystic glow, and the white plaster figures of the Rodin group looked down on the scene from their high place.

A chapter from the Bible in Samoan was read. Now the head of the house came forward, with serious and dignified manner, yes, the former freethinker and scoffer, Robert Louis Stevenson, to say a prayer in English, which he himself had written.

"Aid us, oh Lord," he said, "if it be Thy will, in our concerns. Have mercy on this land and innocent people. Help them who this day contend in disappointment with their frailties. Bless our family, bless our forest house, bless our island helpers. Thou, who has made for us this place of ease and hope, accept and inflame our gratitude; help us to repay, in service one to another, the debt of Thine unmerited benefits and mercies, so that when the period of our stewardship draws to a conclusion, when the windows begin to be darkened, when the bond of the family is to be loosed, there shall be no bitterness of remorse in our farewells."

"Amen," added Robert Louis Stevenson at the end of his prayer, and he was honestly moved, moved by the beautiful sound of his own voice, by the thoughts he had put into words, by the childlike, serious expression of faith on the faces of his Samoan household, who had listened in absolute silence and guessed the meaning of the prayer although they could not understand it. Now they threw themselves with enthusiasm into the singing of a long hymn in Samoan, and they ended with the Lord's Prayer in the language of their country.

"Thy will be done!" Louis thought of death as he bowed his head. "Forgive us our debts as we forgive our debtors." R. L. S. thought of the friend with whom he had quarrelled.

When Stevenson came to Samoa and established his home in Vailima, he started the patriarchal practice of evening prayers for the household to please his pious Presbyterian mother, who was at that time visiting him. Later, when she returned to spend a year in Scotland, the custom was retained, at least for Sunday evenings, because the servants of the house and the plantation, like all Samoans, loved to "make a church," to chant their Samoan hymns and to listen to their chief Tusitala say obviously pious, if not comprehensible, phrases in a solemn tone. This was all in keeping with a semi-princely style of living; it gave Tusitala a standing in the land and increased his moral influence. Even the many Catholics among the staff of Vailima could take no exception to these household prayers in which all mention of strictly denominational matters was carefully avoided. It was only the missionaries of Stevenson's own confession, the Presbyterian Church of Scotland, who found him lacking in zeal and orthodoxy. After the senior Mrs. Stevenson left Samoa, neither Louis nor Fanny nor her children went to church. This was a matter of public knowledge in Samoa and it was the subject of much comment. Nevertheless, he remained on friendly terms with both the numerous Protestant missionaries and the Catholic as well.

Although this erstwhile bohemian was now a tanned and respectable person who made a decorous impression with his religious activities, still it did cause a stir in Apia when the news was spread, one day in April in 1894, that Mr. Stevenson had agreed to take over a Sunday school class of Samoan children and to teach them the Christian religion and Bible history. When Moors heard about it, he made some fierce remarks about petticoat government and apron strings. It was actually a fact that a feminine influence, in addition to a sudden whim, had induced R. L. S. to make his childhood dream come true, and to turn preacher; but it was not the person suspected by his irascible friend. Neither Fanny nor her daughter was particularly church-minded, and neither of them had urged R. L. S. to take a hand in the work of the Sunday school. It would have been more likely that the thought of his mother, who was soon to return to Samoa to stay, might prompt him to do it. She was a faithful daughter of Scottish Covenanters and she would have been overjoyed to hear, when she arrived, that her beloved son was spending his Sabbaths in such a pious and respectable occupation. But to tell the truth, the impulse had come from another direction; it was the smile of the beautiful young girl to whom he had so magnanimously given his birthday, which had really brought him to the point of taking a Sunday school class of Kanaka children.

Anne Ide, who was already generally known as Louise, was the one of the new Chief Justice's three beautiful daughters who received the lion's share of attention from the lieutenants and midshipmen of the visiting men-of-war, not to mention the young clerks in the German Plantations Society. She lived with her father and her two sisters, Adelaide and

Marjorie, in a house which was set on a hill and overlooked Matootna, a suburb of Apia. In contrast to the attitude of his predecessor the present Chief Justice, Henry C. Ide, was on the most friendly terms with Stevenson, and there was a lively social intercourse between their two households. One evening in April, R. L. S. and Belle were invited to dine at the Ides. The other guests were the New Zealander Gurr and his wife Fanua, Tusitala's great friend. Fanua threw her arms around Belle's neck and greeted Tusitala with a teasing remark, indicative of the joking warfare they carried on together.

"How is the Aitu?" asked R. L. S. He liked to assert that Fanua was really identical with Aitu Fafine, the phantom wood-witch on Mt. Vaea. She pouted with her full lips, for as a Samoan she did not like to hear the divinities of the woods and mountains mentioned frivolously. At the same time—and it did not occur to her pretty flower-wreathed head that there was anything contradictory in this—she was a practicing Christian and averse to anything heathen. She sulked for a bit, as Stevenson persisted in calling her Aitu, and reproached him with not believing either in the heathen Aitus or God.

"Thank goodness that the Tamatai Matua is coming back soon; then you will have to be good and go to church."

Tamatai Matua, highborn elderly lady, was the Samoan name for Stevenson's God-fearing mother, the friend of the missionaries.

"Louise" Ide heard what Fanua said and clapped her hands somewhat coyly.

"Oh, Mr. Stevenson, how wonderful! When your mother comes you really must take over one of the classes in my Sunday school. It is such a bore to have to go down there all by myself."

She looked at him with the round eyes of a child. He looked at her with a paternal expression. That was his attitude towards her. He said magnanimously:

"That has nothing at all to do with my mother's arrival. I have for a long time wanted to tell children the beautiful stories of the Bible. As far as I am concerned, I should just as soon make it next Sunday, Louise. Will you speak to Miss Large about it, or shall I?"

The American girl gave him a languishing look. She thought it was too sweet for words to have this famous writer treat her in such a fatherly way, and she wrote numerous letters to her former schoolmates back home in America, raving about R. L. S. until they all nearly died of jealousy.

So it happened that on the very next Sunday this writer of the abominated and sceptical *fin de siècle* school stood in the bare Protestant Mission Church of Apia, before a crowd of naked or only half-clad Kanaka children, who squatted as usual on the floor and stared at him with their great dark eyes, full of shyness but also of the infinitely knowing and shrewd expression which animals of the forest have. The

205

head of the Sunday school was that same Miss Large who had so efficiently organized the hospital in the Public Hall. She introduced Tusitala to the children and put them on their good behaviour; then she went out to another room to save the souls of grownups. Miss Ide was present, but kept respectfully in the background. R. L. S. was attended by one of the half-breed parish assistants, dressed in a loincloth and a Prince Albert coat, who interpreted for him. The time had now come for him to explain all the mysteries of creation to these savage youngsters, who sat on the floor at his feet and stared at him, or who were punching each other or squirming around. When it came to the point, the great teller of tales suddenly felt the golden stream of his stories dry up inside of him; it just vanished. It seemed to him that he was utterly incapable of telling even the old story of Adam and Eve to these little barbarians. He could not do it in his native Scottish tongue, much less in Samoan. If these Sunday school children, whom he was supposed to turn into pious and Christian creatures, could have read his thoughts at this moment they would have had the impression that they were quite unchristian and rather blasphemous. He was just able to hold himself in sufficiently to keep from swearing out loud. He certainly had got himself into a fine mess! It was abominably hot in the church, but he had to be respectable and keep on his velvet jacket. Then, too, he felt the admiring gaze of his "adopted daughter," Miss Ide, as it rested on him. To disgrace himself before her would be frightful.

His brown audience had all of the keen sensitiveness of their age and soon began to feel Tusitala's embarrassment; they reflected it with increasing clearness by becoming more and more restless. He must pull himself together somehow, do something to give proof of tremendous superiority. He grew red in the face, and the veins stood out on his forehead. It was too silly, but he could not think how to make a beginning. Suddenly it came to him. It was a stroke of genius.

"Children," he said, "I think it would be a good idea if you asked me a question about your last lesson. And do you know what? Whoever asks a really good question will receive sixpence, a nice shiny sixpenny piece, with which to buy some candy!"

He looked around with a triumphant air, but the children only stared at him and said never a word.

R. L. S. thought that they had not understood his Samoan, so he asked the interpreter to translate what he had said. He did it but the children remained unmoved. They had suddenly become very quiet. One little fellow, about six years old who had been whispering to his older brother, reached for his big toe, and regarded it silently, thoughtfully. This big brother, who appeared to have arrived at the ripe age of nine, played with a string of shells which dangled over his inflated breadfruit tummy.

So Tusitala increased his already generous offer. Not sixpence, but a whole shilling, would the rich man give to the good boy who would ask him a sensible question.

207

The silence in the church was unbroken, except for the yapping of the little dog who had followed his master into the holy precincts.

Yet the great storyteller, Robert Louis Stevenson, who had been accustomed to hold the cleverest of men and the most beautiful of women spellbound by the magic of his speech, could think of nothing more effective to do than raise his simonist offer once more. It now assumed gigantic proportions. He now promised a shiny half-crown piece, worth five sixpence, with the image of Queen Victoria on it. Only Tusitala, the rich man of Vailima who had an imp in a bottle at home, could dream of making such an incredible offer. It might be described in equivalent terms if one said that Baron Rothschild had offered a million francs for the solution of a crossword puzzle. It was impossible, irresistible; one could not continue to maintain the goggle-eyed silence.

Out of the deep silence in the church there now broke forth a flood of shrill chatter and excited babble of children's voices. The parish assistant, himself greatly excited, tried in vain to restore order. R. L. S. looked around weakly for he found himself suddenly surrounded by a wilderness of little yelling savages who were holding their hands out to him and pulling on his coat. He was helpless, but unexpectedly a solution presented itself. The little fellow who had been playing with his string of shells raised his hand to ask a question. He was Soolevao, the brave child of a chieftain.

The others lapsed into immediate silence and watched their courageous comrade with admiration.

"That is fine," said Tusitala, who had quickly recovered his pedagogic self-possession. "What is your name? Soolevao? Soolevao is now going to tell us what it is that he could not understand in the Bible and which he would like to have explained. So ask your question, Soolevao, and you shall have a nice, shiny half-crown."

To judge by the expression on his face, Soolevao was full of utmost resolution. He remained seated, for it was not proper to stand in the presence of a High Chief of such distinction as Tusitala; one had to remain squatting on one's heels. Then he spoke, pronouncing each word so slowly and distinctly that R. L. S. could understand him without the help of the interpreter. He said:

"We learned in the Sunday school that the illustrious God created the world. But who, O Tusitala, made the High Chief God?"

Robert Louis Stevenson hastily took a half-crown coin from his pocket, gave it to the boy without a word, and abruptly left the church.

Thus ended his attempt at being a preacher in a Sunday school.

The question was answered, in Tusitala's stead, by Miss Large, who of course had the right answer as prescribed by the orthodoxy of the Protestant Church.

The next time that Stevenson was confined to bed with a fever—it was a very small matter, for on the whole he was very well nowadays—it seemed to him that he was really obliged to find his own answer to Soolevao's question. He must create God, and he must do it today. In his feverish state, the novelist Stevenson could not achieve the creation of anything except a character in a novel. It was perfectly clear to him that he was as much created by God as that young Archie Weir had been, bit by bit, created by him.

During a delirious night he became convinced that something was wrong. Had he miscreated God, or had God miscreated him?

The individual episodes, the weaving of the plot of the story, were infinitely charming, but the ending, which anybody could guess right in the middle . . . "it's no good!" exclaimed R. L. S. in a fever of abuse to God. "My guiding spirit has left me. I have no more imagination!" And Soolevao crept out from under the covers to laugh at him until his little swollen belly shook. His laughter shook the bed, the house, the earth. The sick man awoke, drenched with perspiration and groaning.

CHAPTER XIV

THE PAPER CHASE

IT was seldom now that he was ill. In the second half of 1894 Robert Louis Stevenson, or perhaps it was Tusitala, was at the zenith of his happiness and of his life—Tusitala the beautifully carved figurehead on the bow of the bark which carried the adventurous poet over the seas of his dreams. The figurehead in the bow and the captain of the ship were so alike that they could be taken for each other, except that the former was much more colourful, more imposing, more robustly built, and he was made of wood.

The civil war between the parties of the rival chiefs went right on in Samoa even after the defeat of Mataafa. Tusitala's friend was a prisoner on the island of Jaluit, but this had not contributed either to King Laupepa's popularity or power. In Mataafa's place another rival had arisen in the person of Tamasese. He and his partisans were concentrated in the mountains of the interior of Upolu, beyond the reach of the guns on the foreign battleships. From time to time he made exceptions in his way of life and came down to build fortresses on the beach. Whereupon one or the other of the foreign men-of-war would fire on the rebel stronghold. Then Tamasese, with the perennial politeness of a Samoan, would send a message to the commander of the ship suggesting that he need not waste his powder as there was no one left in the fortress.

Sometimes, of an evening when they were dancing in Vailima, to the music of an accordion—this was the usual evening occupation as long as the Austrian Count von Wurmbrand was there—warriors with blackened faces would appear suddenly on the veranda and ask for refreshment. After this was given, they would go on their way. In spite of the fact that the Apia newspaper, which had now passed into the hands of the Germans, was continually asserting that R. L. S. was smuggling arms into Samoa, actually he hardly had a single serviceable revolver in the house—after the incident with Laupepa he had had enough of revolvers—and no one would have dreamed of molesting him. He made practically no comment on the struggle between Tamasese and Malietoa Laupepa; he was equally indifferent to both. The civil war, which was not particularly sanguinary but still senseless and demoralizing, went on, while the "protecting" powers interfered continually but ineffectively because they never could agree on anything. The only fact which was now clear to them all was Laupepa's unfitness. Even the Germans, whose influence was steadily increasing, while showing displeasure over the doings of the rebel Tamasese, began to manifest a kind of mildness towards Mataafa. The day was to come when Samoa would be officially annexed by Germany, and in that colony Mataafa was to rule, not as King but still as ranking Chief. For the time being he had to remain on Jaluit, but his partisans were less and less severely pursued. They were let out of prison and all Tusitala's friends went free.

Stevenson wrote a few more letters to the *Times* and *Daily Chronicle* on behalf of Mataafa and those who were exiled with him, but they lacked the passion and sharpness of his earlier communications on the subject of Samoan politics. He remained a loyal friend to Mataafa, but he had lost his faith in the possibility of salvaging the national independence of the Polynesian peoples, and he had even ceased to fight for it himself.

Towards the end of June things began to stir in Vailima. Graham Balfour had come back to Samoa and was visiting the Stevensons again. Austin Strong, Belle's young son, was home from school in San Francisco, and was making things lively around the house. The winter sportsman Lloyd Osbourne finally came back from New Zealand, bringing Louis' mother, whom he had met in Auckland on her way back from Scotland. The elder Mrs. Stevenson—or "Aunt Maggie," as everyone called her—had come with all of her belongings and intended to settle down permanently with her beloved Lou. These belongings included her clothing, her linen and a supply of widow's bonnets and veils in the

213

style of Queen Victoria, to last her the rest of her life. These she wore even in the tropics of Samoa. She had also packed up and sent on to Apia, in thirty-eight huge cases, all of her massive, early Victorian furniture from her home in Heriot Row. This was the furniture which had surrounded R. L. S. as he was growing up. There were the stiff, upholstered armchairs into which he had climbed when, as a child dressed in a clergyman's robe and bands, he had delighted his pious mother with his long sermons. These chairs were also the heirlooms of Aunt Maggie's family, the Balfours. When the mountainous pile of cases was unloaded on the beach, soon after the old lady's arrival, the whole of Samoa practically stood on its head with excitement. The wildest of rumours were current as to the magnificence and richness of the furniture, especially concerning a certain large mirror, such as Samoa had never seen before. Although these furnishings were in reality quite ordinary, bourgeois, and lacking in comfort, still they gave an air of solid respectability to the great hall at Vailima which the home of R. L. S., the bohemian litterateur, had lacked, and besides he was glad to see them all again.

They now took their meals around a massive mahogany table. Even when there were no guests, the combined Stevenson and Balfour family numbered no less than seven members; there were the Stevensons, mother and son, there was Fanny Stevenson with her son Lloyd Osbourne, Isobel Strong and her son Austin, and Graham Balfour. The recognized

214

head of this flourishing clan, whose Samoan household was dressed in tartans of Royal Stuart plaid, could certainly not feel lonely any more, even if he lacked all outside society— which was not by any means the case.

Certainly not. For another British man-of-war was in the harbour of Apia, Her Majesty's cruiser, *Curaçao,* and the Stevensons made friends with the officers and men more quickly and thoroughly than they had done earlier with those of the *Katoomba.* Shortly after the arrival of the vessel, the commander invited R. L. S. to take a little cruise on board, over to the island of Manua, which was one of the outlying parts of the Samoan Archipelago. By some fortuitous over-sight of colonial diplomacy, this island had, up to this point, maintained its complete independence under the gentle rule of a beautiful, half-caste Queen. Naturally it was high time that a man-of-war should go there to establish order. When R. L. S. came home, a few days later, he was full of Manua and its Queen, but he was even more excited by life on board a warship. His feelings as a Briton and as a romanticist had been aroused by the elaborate manoeuvres, when everything happened almost as though they were actually in a battle, and by many other incidents. While he was on board, he had asked an unbroken stream of questions, with especial bearing on naval terminology, which he wanted to use in a novel of naval life. He had been avid in picking up slang expressions from the young midshipmen. With this end in view, he drank his morning chocolate with the middies, but for afternoon tea he went to the officers' messroom. Everything fascinated and delighted him, including even a calling down he received from the captain for accidentally intruding on a space reserved for the officer on duty. The captain's gruff remarks gave him the pleasant feeling that somehow he "belonged."

All this hospitality shown to the plantation owner of Vailima must naturally be returned. First of all the Scots aboard the *Curaçao* found their way to Vailima "with the instinct of homing pigeons," as R. L. S. described it. Then he offered Vailima as a sanatorium to the captain and the ship's doctor, by the name of Hoskyn, suggesting that they send any sick men out there to convalesce. Soon the Stevensons' front veranda was known as the "Curaçao Club," because of the free way in which the officers of the *Curaçao*, as well as those of the two German vessels lying in the harbour, came and went. Naturally the Vailima family took part in the big ball arranged by the officers of the *Curaçao*, which went off with great success. Nor could they refuse an invitation, brought to them a few days later by a deputation of petty officers, to come to a ball to be given by the crew. Even young Austin was asked to go along, for he already had a little boy's intimacy with the sailors.

Then there was Austin's birthday to be celebrated. A child's party was arranged and, in a spirit of innocent mischief, the young midshipmen of the *Curaçao* were invited. In order to salve the feelings of these young "officers and gentlemen," R. L. S. saw to it that all of the prettiest half-caste girls who were available in Samoa were also asked to the party. Under these conditions the midshipmen need not be embarrassed to give themselves up to the childish pleasures of a little boy's birthday party; they could play the parts of sophisticated young men and Don Juans and be gay and foolish with the girls.

This was the year when, more than ever before in Vailima, they celebrated birthdays and holidays. It almost seemed that no opportunity for interrupting R. L. S.'s work was allowed to slip by. Under the strict supervision of his secretary, Belle, he pursued his writing conscientiously, but it was done only in the intervals between festivities. They had begun in February by celebrating Washington's birthday in honour of Fanny Van de Grift Stevenson's American patriotism. They had a gala meal with little American flags among the decorations on the table. After that, how could they ignore Queen Victoria's birthday in May and not put little Union Jacks on the festive board? Close on the heels of that came Independence Day on the fourth of July, and the French national holiday on the fourteenth. For Stevenson alway felt that he had two countries, his own and La Belle France, and it would have been unthinkable that he should let that day go by without adorning his table with little French flags. As there was no other Frenchman available with whom to celebrate the Fall of the Bastille, R. L. S. again invited the Catholic Bishop of Oceania to a meal. This time the prelate was so enthusiastic about the excellent soup that when Talolo came in under pretext of serving the after-dinner coffee, which was not his office (in reality he wanted to kneel to kiss the Bishop's ring and to receive his compliments on the art of his cooking), his Grace immediately volunteered a specially broad dispensation for his sins. These popish practices must have made Aunt Maggie's good Calvinistic grey hair stand on end under her widow's cap. However, she had the consolation of being able to invite to her own birthday party those friends who were of her faith, the Protestant missionaries and their wives. On that occasion little Austin Strong—who was really her step-great-grandson, although he called her Aunt—was obliged to recite a long, long poem, full of many long, long words, which R. L. S. with mischievous impishness had composed. He had made it difficult on purpose, so that the boy would learn how to memorize and recite. The teasing author listened with a grin on his face, and when Austin stuck it out to the end he called out: "Bravo!"

Any cause and any pretext were used to have a party. Throughout the hot tropical evenings, rows of flaming torches flanked the garden gate at Vailima. The natives came in droves to see the guests arrive, to take their horses and hitch them to the posts. Inside the house the great mahogany table was laid, as it had been in the days when Robert Louis Stevenson's grandfather, the lighthouse builder, had entertained his friends. There was room to seat twenty guests around this venerable board. On it lay the heavy solid silver of the Stevenson family, their good glass and china. The

218

servants who waited on the table may have looked like savages, but they were well trained to serve the marvellous meals which the good Talolo created out of the recipes of many foreign lands and peoples, under the personal supervision of his culinarily gifted mistress. From the wall above the carved bookcase that dour old Scot, the lighthouse builder, looked down with ever-solemn expression on these extraordinary Oceano-European dinner parties. But once, when the beautiful Fanua climbed up on a chair and draped a garland of Samoan flowers around the old fellow's angular Scotch head, R. L. S. said he could have sworn that Grandfather began to smile. After dinner dancing was started on the waxed floor in the hall, under the direction of a real Count, as *maître de plaisir*. They danced the *schottische* and the Johann Strauss waltzes from Vienna.

It was considered most unfortunate that Robert, Count von Wurmbrand-Stuppach, the perennial boarder, the dancing master, the super-cowboy, and jack-of-all-trades of Vailima, should for some quite obscure reasons feel impelled to disappear from Upolu and go to visit some neighboring island at the very moment when another Count was expected to arrive. This new Count also originated in the Austro-Hungarian Empire, was also a former Imperial and Royal Cavalry officer and undoubtedly must have known Count von Wurmbrand extremely well. On July 3, in accordance with advance advices, the steam yacht *Tolna* arrived in the roads of Apia. The owner and the captain was Count Festetics de

Tolna. He had married the daughter of a millionaire in San Francisco, and their adventurous journey on their tiny boat was in the nature of a honeymoon. There was a huge stack of letters for them at the post office in Apia, where everyone saw the mail intended for everyone else. Count von Wurmbrand, too, must have seen those letters and realized that the *Tolna* was soon due to arrive. Yet, apparently he had not felt that he could wait for the coming of his travelling fellow-nobleman, comrade in arms and countryman—if one could say that in the Dual Monarchy an Austrian and a Hungarian really were countrymen. Only two days before the yacht came in, he had left a letter for the new arrivals, and disappeared as completely as though he had been swallowed up by the ocean.

The man who climbed aboard the *Tolna* to deliver the other Count's letter to Count Festetics had no coat on nor any shoes; his linen trousers were rolled up to his thin knees, showing the white skin which betrayed his European origin even from a distance. While Count Festetics opened and read the letter, the man stood before him in an expectant attitude, and the Count was considering whether or not to give this beachcomber a tip or a drink. We have no information as to what the letter contained except an invitation. Count von Wurmbrand urged Festetics and his wife to make a call at Vailima, where the Stevensons would be happy to have them as their guests.

Robert Louis Stevenson! The name was familiar even to a

former Lieutenant of Hungarian Hussars, retired, notwith-standing the fact that Festetics, later on describing his friend-ship with Stevenson in the inevitable book on his South Seas voyage, invariably referred to the most famous Scottish writer of his age as a "great American."

"Please, will you have the kindness to inform Mr. Steven-son that I shall consider it a great honour to make his ac-quaintance?" said the trig young Count to the waiting beach-comber. "I shall come to him today."

"That is fine," said the beachcomber. "But you have al-ready made his acquaintance; I am Robert Louis Stevenson."

During this whole time, while Count Festetics was reading the letter, and R. L. S. was waiting at his side, a struggle had been going on inside Tusitala: Should he, or should he not, ask the Count what the letter contained in addition to the invitation? It was obvious that Wurmbrand was avoiding a meeting with Festetics. The honeymooning owner of the yacht would probably know the story of the nobleman beach-comber, and R. L. S. had long suspected that his bearded friend and pet Count might be an interesting subject for a novelist. But the discreet gentleman in his nature triumphed on this occasion over the inquisitive writer. The question was not asked, and Stevenson's readers were never to know how it came about that a former officer of the Imperial and Royal Austro-Hungarian Cavalry had turned into a gaoler, a danc-ing master and a cowboy, out in the South Seas.

Since they missed their own Count so grievously at Vailima, they were all the more cordial in their welcome to the new Count with his rich, young and very American wife. There is some snobbery in every Briton, and R. L. S. was no exception to the rule. His hospitable house was open to everyone, to common sailors as well as to noblemen; but when a Count came, they did make a little more of a fuss. Their aristocratic guest from faraway Hungary saw Vailima in all its glory and was properly impressed. To this pampered gentleman accustomed to life in Paris, after his long cruise through the South Seas, this house out in the midst of the wild bushland compared favourably with the most elegant houses on the Avenue de Villiers. At night, when the lights shone on the verandas, balconies and galleries, all trimmed with flowers and vines, it made him think of paintings by Paolo Veronese of Venetian nocturnal festivals. Then, in the stable of Vailima, the ex-hussar found what he had missed most out in that part of the world—horses. In Vailima the American Countess met some of her compatriots, the lovely Misses Ide, and also the Samoan lady Fanua, who, to confuse matters, was also Mrs. Gurr, the wife of a white gentleman. She was the one who gave the Countess and the three Ide girls lessons in Siva dancing, where the dancers all sit in a long row on the grass, swathed in garlands of heavily scented flowers, and make motions with the hands and arms and upper part of the body intended to convey the meaning of the Samoan songs which accompany them.

There were other occasions even more characteristically

222

Samoan. One was when Fanua's father, Seumanutafa (the Count heard and wrote down only "Sumana"), the ranking chief of Apia and a friend of Tusitala, invited the house of Vailima, with all of their guests, also the Ides, the officers of the *Curaçao,* and many English and American notables in the colony, to join him and his fellow chiefs in a great picnic. It was held at the Falls of the Vaisingana river, which the natives used as a water slide. If one was a bold enough swimmer, one slid skillfully through the rocks, down over foaming falls, into the lovely pool at their feet, which was surrounded by ferns and blooming lianas. In this warm and transparent pool they all swam together, the midshipmen from the *Curaçao,* the young Samoan girls with their dusky golden skin and the Samoan warriors with their tattooed legs. In swimming the young English seamen were hard put to it to compete with the Kanakas with any credit to Old England. After the gay water sports, they ate their luncheon out of doors, all sitting around on the ground on an elevation which had been strewn with red flower petals. Delicately woven baskets of leaves served as plates, and fingers were used for forks. The fare consisted of roast pig, pigeons, chickens, breadfruit and taro, which was buried and baked in a pit. There were also delectable crabs, crayfish and remarkable puddings made of coconut. Everyone was in a jovial mood and Seumanutafa's young warriors were just preparing to sing a bloodthirsty war song, albeit their intentions were of a most pacific nature, when who should suddenly break in on the gay festivities but some real enemies! It was a military patrol of Tamasese rebels, armed and covered with black war paint, who appeared at the top of the waterfall. They sent an old woman down to act as herald. She stepped into the midst of the picnic, looking like some fury, waved her arms about like a mad woman, beat her emaciated breast and began to scream.

"What is she screaming about?" asked Countess Festetics, somewhat alarmed.

"Oh, nothing at all," said Tusitala. "She is yelling 'Your enemies are hungry too! Give them of your abundance!' "

Whereupon the chieftain Seumanutafa sent a whole roast pig and other good things to the enemy patrol. Nor had he been in the least surprised by the incident; it was all part of the customary chivalrous practices among warriors in Samoa.

When the guest of honour in a house is a young cavalryman, the host feels it incumbent on him to offer also some entertainment more congenial to him than dances and picnics. R. L. S. had one obsession which had haunted him all his life. It was the desire to hunt a fox like any healthy Englishman. Now he felt strong enough to gratify it, for during these months he had been feeling outrageously well. He had even dared to play tennis with Anne Ide, and as a result he had had only a minor hemorrhage. He was sure that now he could safely ride in a fox hunt. The only drawback was that with Samoa's complete lack of mammalian fauna, there were no foxes to hunt nor any deer. Nothing was left to do except organize a paper chase. One Sunday in August was the day chosen. And that they should have picked the Lord's Day, when all good Presbyterians ought to go to church, was the subject of much comment in the pious missionary circles of Samoa. One may well assume that the feelings of the elder Mrs. Stevenson, who had so recently seen her son appear in the worthy role of a Sunday school teacher, were now outraged by this breaking of the Sabbath, held so sacred in Scotland. Yet on the credit side of the ledger, she was inordinately proud that her always ailing son, her dear Lou, was physically able to stand all sorts of tests, and that he was able to be in the saddle for a whole day, riding over hill and dale like the—no, not like the devil; Aunt Maggie would never have used so wicked a word!

Since no God-fearing Briton could be persuaded to go hunting on a Sunday, Stevenson invited several young clerks from the German Plantations Society to join him, Lloyd and Count Festetics. They all met at the Vaiele Plantation, agreed on the rules of the game and rode off.

When the hunt started, Stevenson was completely happy. His brown pony Jack sensed this, as a horse always feels his rider's mood, and behaved himself to perfection. He took his master over stick and stone, through underbrush and coco plantations, without stumbling, without faltering, without falling. If Stevenson himself, who was a rather mediocre pathfinder, had not overlooked the slip of paper and so missed the trail, he might have succeeded in winning, over the celebrated huntsman Count Festetics de Tolna, and brought home the "fox." As it was, he outrode most of the others and suddenly found himself alone in a broad clearing. He came around a large boulder and, looking up, saw in the distance the outline of a familiar mountain. It was the top of Mt. Vaea, and with a good field glass he could have seen the very spot he had chosen for his future burial place. Perhaps that is why the thought crossed Robert Louis Stevenson's mind, as he reined in his horse and listened to the distant thud of galloping hoofs ahead: Whom am I pursuing? Can it be death?

He brushed the thought aside and rode on, but Jack, to whom his mood had been communicated—or did he sense something strange, uncanny?—Jack began to stumble. R. L. S. moderated his pace and pretended to himself that it was on account of the stumbling, yet actually it was because he would not, for anything, have overtaken the rider ahead of him. He was overwhelmed by some superstitious sense of which he could not rid himself. Perhaps it was a subconscious memory of his mother's warning against going hunting on Sunday, for one who has been raised in puritanical ways never quite sheds them. He rode so slowly that the sound of the thundering hoofs ahead of him faded away entirely, but then he became aware of others which were coming up on him from behind. He was seized with a feeling of terrible foreboding: no, it is behind me, *that* is where death is. He was about to spur his horse on quickly, but Jack had already spurted forward and again he could hear the sound of an invisible rider ahead of him, spurring an invisible horse through the stones of a gully.

Now Robert Louis Stevenson was in the anguishing grip of an imaginary terror; terror rode before as well as after him. He suddenly realized that he was riding a hopeless race against death, that he had been doing this all of his life, and especially out here in Samoa. Whether he rode breathlessly in paper chases, or spent himself in boyish games, or in what he might call work, it was all one; it was all a senseless, fearful chase behind a galloping death who was the fox, while that same death pursued him like a baying hound snapping at his horse's heels. What escape could there be? Everything that he had done in all these recent months was really just a grotesque paper chase. Yet no matter how hard he hunted, how feverishly he worked, he could never catch up with death . . . and meantime death was catching up with him. . . .

The sound of hoofs behind him grew constantly clearer. He did not turn around, nor did he spur Jack on; rather he relied on the horse's own instinct.

Lloyd Osbourne had remained behind his stepfather on purpose so that he could keep an eye on him, for he was not a little worried by the horseback riding excesses of this wilful invalid. The result was that although Lloyd was a good rider

227

he came in fourth, right after R. L. S., who was third. It was a sporting accomplishment and received the discriminating praise of the ex-hussar Festetics, who had, of course, won the race himself. He did not notice that R. L. S. was extremely pale as he dismounted, but this did not escape Lloyd Osbourne.

Two days after the paper chase, Stevenson wrote to his friend Sidney Colvin that he was tempted to give up literature and devote himself to planting cacao because the exercise in the open did him so much good. Yet where would he find anyone to pay him the ten pounds a day which he must have to run Vailima?

Several days after writing that extravagant letter, he aroused the keen displeasure of his secretary Isobel by telling her, rather curtly, that he was giving up the work on *St. Ives,* which was almost finished, to devote himself exclusively to his great Scottish novel, *Weir of Hermiston.* Belle could not understand him; but he had heard the sound of an invisible horseman riding after him and he dared not lose any more time.

The whole book was now so clear in his mind that he could almost reach out and touch it!

There are the two Weirs at Hermiston, father and son. The father is the Lord Justice-Clerk of Scotland, made of iron, and inflexible, like a metal statue of Justice. The son is soft, human and weak in a rather lovable way. While

Archie Weir is a student at the Law School in Edinburgh—for where else should the son of a great judge be studying?—he impulsively commits a youthful indiscretion. It is nothing wicked, not even particularly blameworthy: his father, as immutable as usual, has just handed down a death sentence and Archie goes into the "Spec.," the students' debating society and makes a speech against capital punishment. (Many of the similar radical speeches which young Louis Stevenson made in the "Speculative Society" must have displeased his own strict and puritanical father!) Lord Hermiston hears, of course, about the incident. Naturally he is convinced that anyone who harbours such views is unfit ever to sit on the judge's bench in Scotland. From his Cato-like point of view his son is a hopeless failure, and he sends him into exile on the country estate of the family. This is where the subsequent scenes of the drama are played.

Whereas Stevenson had allowed the depressing seriousness of the puritanical atmosphere in old Scotland to overlay the early chapters, as though he were drawing his pictures with a slate pencil on a grey stone tablet, he now allowed himself a little gayety in the following chapters. He drew Kirstie Elliott, the housekeeper at Hermiston, with affectionate humour, as a type of Scottish womanhood. In contrast to her harsh, resolute dourness, he set another woman's portrait, a more lovable one. This was of her niece, the young Kirstie, who was also an Elliott, carved out of the same hard wood, daughter of an ancient race of shepherds, fighters and

229

border brigands. She meets the Laird's son and the first sparks of a flaming love bring light into Archie's life. The joyless winter on the moors along the Scottish-English border is transformed into a lovely succession of unforgettable days. Archie Weir forgets everything, the boredom of his lonely life, the provincial society of squires and dull local worthies who seek to draw him into their alcohol-reeking diversions. Hosts of characters, sketched with the sure hand of a master, people the pages of this fragment of a novel; all the countryside of Scotland comes to life, the landscape so beautiful in its melancholy barrenness, and the corresponding human beings, their customs, prejudices, virtues, shortcomings.

" 'Mephistofeles' makes his entrance," R. L. S. wrote at the head of the seventh chapter. In the sixth he had put one of the tenderest love scenes in any romantic novel, in which Kirstie had sung to her friend the wonderful ballad about the "old stony cold Elliotts of yore":

> "Auld, auld Elliotts, clay-cauld Elliotts, dour,
> bauld Elliotts of auld."

Then he had described the wild Elliotts of that time, Kirstie's brothers, and given the impression that they were no less cold and bold than their ancestors; they were shepherds too, and determined to go the limit against an enemy, and in defense of family honour or of a friend.

And now—Mephistopheles. He takes the form of Frank

Innes, Archie's dissipated companion, who steps between the lovers and attempts to debauch Kirstie.

R. L. S. had not come to the point of writing down the ultimate tragic scenes of his great novel, when Archie quarrels with Frank, and kills him by the "Weaver's Rock," when Archie's own father sits in judgment over him and, as inflexible as an old Roman, with unmoved face pronounces the death sentence on his only son, the last scion of the Weirs of Hermiston. These great scenes were still to be written, as well as the ending, where the "Four Black Brothers" were to abduct Archie by force out of his prison, and free him and his Kirstie from all terrors. . . .

The foundations for this epic structure were all laid. Now the time had come to crown it with a roof. This was when Robert Louis Stevenson, engaged in the interesting and socially charming sport of a paper chase, heard the gallop of a phantom horse close on his trail.

CHAPTER XV

THANKSGIVING

AS the month of August, 1894, drew to a close, the stormy waves of Samoan politics appeared to have somewhat abated. Tamasese's rising also had failed; he had not been able to assert himself in the face of opposition from the warships of the Great Powers. So he concluded, or pretended to conclude, a peace with Laupepa. Moreover, those chiefs of the Mataafa party who were still captive in the strange prison camp near Apia, one day sent a formal act of submission to the King, and were released on that basis. Instead of going home, they held a big council, drank kava and passed certain resolutions which had to do with Tusitala, their friend, when they were in trouble. And then one Monday morning, just as R. L. S. was settling down to dictate a few more pages of *Weir of Hermiston,* he saw, more to his surprise than pleasure, nine chieftain worthies crossing the lawn towards his house. He realized at once that this meant some long speeches, and a large bowl of kava—in other words his whole morning was hopelessly done for. But he had no recourse except to put a good face on these ceremonial matters and to receive the deputation with all due unction.

Of the members of the family, Fanny was in Apia, where she had gone to visit in order to avoid the risk of communicating her cold to Louis, and the senior Mrs. Stevenson had sailed over to Lulumoenga with some missionaries, to the opening of a mission school, an occasion which she could not think of missing. The remaining members grouped themselves picturesquely in the smoking room around the head of their clan, Tusitala, as the former prisoners filed in and sat down in a great semicircle on the floor. They were headed by the old chief Poè, Talolo's father-in-law. He had been seriously sick while in prison, and both Tusitala and Fanny had done a great deal for him in the way of friendly assistance. The idea, which was now to be put forward with so much ceremony, had originated with him. The other chiefs in the group were: Lelei, Salevao, Teleso, Tupuola, Lotofogo, Tupuola Amaile, Muliaiga, Ifopo, Fatialofa and Mataafà. In spite of the similarity of names, this latter was not in any way related to the family of Mataafa.

The chieftains had, of course, brought along an official Talking Man, who, after the usual expressions of polite compliments were out of the way, came to the object of their call: these ten chiefs had been pardoned by King Laupepa, but they had not been required, as were the other Mataafa chieftains and their followers, to work on the roads for a certain length of time to round out their punishment. This was a type of work which the Samoans particularly resented, and that was why it had been imposed on the first of the Mataafa

233

partisans who had been freed. Now these last ten chiefs to come out of prison had come to the incredible conclusion that they would volunteer their services to do some of this much detested work. They would build a road, but it would not be at the behest of or for the benefit of King Laupepa. They had come to Tusitala to say to him: you were our friend and our protector when we were in trouble. Now that we have our freedom back again, we do not want to go home and enjoy it in peace until we have done something for you. We know that the road to your High Chief palace in Vailima is not a good one; in bad weather it is impassable. We and our people want to work on it and make it into a good road so that it may be a joy to you and serve to remind you of us.

R. L. S. had been disturbed during his working hours, and he was not in the best of humour. He had heard this friendly offer with mixed feelings. As he knew the Kanakas of the South Seas, the real meaning of this proposal was that he provide for a number of workmen, who might well be of doubtful capacity, with tools, generous amounts of food and unlimited kava, and really to pay them for their work in the guise of giving them presents. He had often pondered the question of whether he should have the bad road to his house from Apia improved. But he was chary of undertaking it at this very moment when he was heartily sick of earning his daily bread and when he wanted to devote himself entirely to his greatest book and to his health without any regard for quick money-making.

234

But here the Talking Man's tone changed. Up to this point he had used the wordy, formal expressions which were his official stock in trade. Now it was as though a mask fell, and his own individual human face was revealed. He did not speak of gratitude, for the Samoan does not say: "I am grateful to you." He says very simply: "I love you." This was what he now said to Tusitala in his own name as well as that of the other chiefs, and he went on with most unusual warmth of expression to the effect that his name was always in their prayers, and that they would never forget what he did for them while they were in captivity and that they were going to build the road for him entirely as a free gift. Tusitala was not to give any gifts, nor any food; their supplies would be brought by boat from the more fertile parts of the island. The only thing that the Vailima plantation would be asked to supply would be the tools.

R. L. S. suddenly felt that these people really meant what they said, and a warm emotion surged through him. This offer of so great a gift, made with such friendly feelings, had to be accepted in a generous way. It was no small thing for the men of Samoa to volunteer to do a piece of work which they looked upon as degrading. Under the influence of the whites, Laupepa's government had brought every possible pressure to bear and yet had been unable to achieve the construction of any really good road on the island of Upolu. And here were these chiefs, freely offering to build the much needed road to Vailima as a "mea alofa," as a gift of love to him, Tusitala.

His thoughts turned to that great old friend of his: You see, Sir George, I have not lived among the Samoans in vain. I really seem to have accomplished something for them, or they would never be so grateful.

Out loud his words were: "And we shall name this way 'The Road of the Loving Hearts'!"

The work on the road was begun as soon as Fanny, looking rather pale but no longer a carrier of germs, came home. The very next morning old Poè appeared with a gang of strong young men. They were not exactly the sons of High Chiefs, but they had evidently been carefully chosen for their capacity for work. To start them off, Tusitala had a huge bowl of kava set up at the scene of operations, and they went through some of the usual and inevitable speeches before falling to work in earnest. The chiefs had decided to do the thing in a truly generous manner and to lay the road thirty feet wide. Many trees had to be felled, great boulders hauled away, much underbrush burned. All in all, it was a difficult piece of work, yet it was accomplished with a rapidity nothing short of magic for a tropical land, and the day quickly drew near when the opening of the road could be foreseen.

Before that, there was still Belle's birthday to be celebrated. This was done by giving a dance at the house for a party of thirty, including the officers of the *Curaçao*. In addition, the chiefs who were overseeing the building of the road came uninvited to stare with wide eyes at the strange and mysterious rites executed by the Papalangi. There was one "war dance," called the "Highland Fling," which made a special impression on them and drew great applause from these native friends of the household. It was long after midnight when they all, Europeans, Americans and Kanakas, joined hands, forming a long chain, and began to sing "Auld Lang Syne." Stevenson's mother kept hours considered proper to her age and had gone to her room promptly at ten o'clock. From her bed she heard the song, and its Scotch tones touched her so unbearably with homesickness that she would have given anything to go down to the hall in her nightgown, to join hands with her son, who so happily had been restored to normal life—including dancing, tennis playing, and riding. But she stayed in her bed, singing to herself the wistful lines which always bring tears to the eyes of a real Scot when he is truly happy. Robert Louis Stevenson's puritanical mother was so deeply grateful to her Calvinistic God!

There was someone else at this time who was thankful to the God of the missionaries, and to all of the old gods of Samoa, but especially to Tusitala: this was Elinga. He had come out from under an anaesthetic, and beside him stood Tusitala, holding his brown hand. The ship's doctor from the *Curaçao* laid aside his knife, and at first Elinga could hardly believe that the great lump he had carried on his back all his life was really gone.

237

Elinga was an important member of the Tusitala clan. He had a long list of offices and functions, but his main occupation was as laundryman. He had been born a High Chief, but in Samoa as in ancient Greece, only the perfect in body were looked upon as fully worthy of high office. He had never been able to claim the succession, with all of its titles and perquisites, for how could he be looked up to, a man with a repulsive cyst the size of a child's head, on his back? This deformity had affected his character. He was forever making gibes intended to get people to laugh at his own misfortune. Yet Tusitala's beautiful, half-naked followers at Vailima hated this creature, who was sometimes servile and at other times full of biting scorn. Nor was he happy among the others who worked for Tusitala; so R. L. S. had solved the problem by letting him live alone in Apia and act as Vailima's emissary there. In his tiny establishment he took care of the laundry and stabled any horses that were left in town; he also did all kinds of errands.

For a long time R. L. S. and Fanny had been trying to persuade the poor fellow to allow this ugly but not malignant tumour to be taken off. Dr. Hoskyn, of the *Curaçao,* maintained that it could be removed quite easily and without any danger. But Elinga was not convinced about the medical art of the Papalangis. He was quite sure that a Samoan has not only a skin different from a white man but different organs under that skin. He insisted that his hump was connected by secret strands with his heart, and that he must surely die if they were disturbed. But Tusitala was so earnest in his entreaty that Elinga finally decided to die for him if that could give him any pleasure.

So he prepared his little beehive hut of woven cane for his approaching demise. He laid his fine mats on the ground and invited his relatives to be present at his execution. It was a regular feast day. While they were in the process of drinking kava, Stevenson, Fanny and the doctor rode up. Elinga came out in front of his hut to meet them. He was ashen with fright, but his bearing was brave, and today no scurrilous remarks passed his lips. He helped his mistress Aolele down from her horse, and led his guests into his house, which gleamed with cleanliness. Then he laid himself down with resignation on a mat, amid the mournful murmurings of his relatives who were clustered around the walls, and waited for death to come. On one side of him stood the doctor in his white coat, and on the other was Tusitala, who was to assist the doctor and help to put the chloroform mask over Elinga's face. As he was going under, Elinga muttered, in his beach-English: "I belong Tusitala, I belong Tusitala. I no damned coward!"

Now, when he woke up and found that the unbelievable was really true and, with the exception of a small scar, his back was perfectly smooth, that he could now retrieve all of his noble titles and trappings, be broke out into a joyful paean. He composed a long song, "The Song of the Hump," which was destined to achieve great popularity among the

Samoan islands. And along with his hump the defects in his character practically disappeared. He no longer played the dwarfish, subservient, malicious fool. He held himself straight and with pride. Moreover, he dyed his hair bright red like a Samoan dandy, and curled it like a gentleman of fashion in ancient Greece. He was like a redeemed prince in a fairy tale when he arrived in Vailima, scented with ointment and sandalwood powder, and at the head of a train of followers. But when he stood once more before Tusitala, he became the hunchback again; he bound a coconut on his back, which was to represent the vanished cyst. In the presence of Tusitala and his family, who sat around him on the veranda, he re-enacted the happy drama of his liberation. His followers sat on the ground in a circle and clapped their hands in rhythmic accompaniment, as he recited, sang and danced his song about his hump. First he was Elinga, the despised, humpbacked fool of other days; he made grimaces, and turned handsprings. Then the coconut fell from his back and he became quite another Elinga, tall and proud, who thumped his chest as if it were a drum and thundered out his song.

"O Tusitala," he sang, "when you came to us here I was ugly and I was poor. Harsh people made fun of me, despised me. All I had to eat was grass, all I had to wear was a skirt of leaves. I had nothing with which to cover up my hateful body. But now, O Tusitala, now I am beautiful. My body is strong and healthy and my noble name once more belongs to me. All this, O Tusitala, I owe to you. My life is wholly yours; I shall serve you till I die."

The solemn opening of the "Road of the Loving Hearts" was turned into a kind of apotheosis of Tusitala; through it the names of Tusitala and Samoa were for all time inextricably bound together.

The ceremony itself, which took place in the early days of October, was simple enough and consisted only of nailing a wooden signboard on a large tree at the entrance of the new road. The text on it had been composed by the Samoan chiefs themselves. It read:

"Considering the great love of Tusitala in his loving care of us in our distress in the prison, we have therefore prepared a splendid gift. It shall never be muddy, it shall endure forever, this road that we have dug."

The real ceremony took place afterwards on the veranda at Vailima. It was a great and wonderful festival, memorable for all time in the annals of Samoa. It almost seemed as though everything to which Robert Louis Stevenson had aspired as Tusitala, had been realized: the reconciliation of the Samoans among themselves, and with the whites who lived among them. Almost all of the official dignitaries of the colony put in an appearance; the new Chief Justice, the new President of the Council, the American consul-general, the English and the American land commissioners, and more than fifty Samoan guests of high rank.

Seumanutafa, ranking chief of Apia, represented the party of King Laupepa at this great feast of reconciliation, and he brought along three beautiful virgins of his own distinguished family so that the kava ceremonies could be carried out with strict adherence to the ancient traditions of Samoa; for on this occasion there was no intention of imitating any English customs; only men were to be called to partake of the kava. The first official speech after the kava drinking was made by Seumanutafa: he spoke in the name of the victorious party, but in terms of most chivalrous courtesy towards those who had been beaten and who had only recently emerged from prison. They had delegated the chief Mataafà, whose name was so like that of their beloved and still banished leader, to speak for them. So Mataafà responded to the speech of the King's party on behalf of the Mataafa party. He returned courtesy for courtesy and even added a few words of loyal acknowledgment and thanks to the King who had pardoned him and those who had shared his destiny. But all the real words of affection were for Tusitala. Then came the great event of the day: Tusitala's speech of thanks for the generous gift, the "Road of the Loving Hearts."

R. L. S. had prepared his address with great care and had had it translated into Samoan by one of the missionaries, who gave to it all of the classic flourishes of the High Chief language. He read his speech first in English, pronouncing every word slowly and clearly. Then he had Lloyd, who was the official herald of the house of Vailima, read the Samoan translation.

It was a beautiful speech, and one worthy of the occasion. The words of thanks in it were few but full of cordiality. Then Tusitala addressed himself to the chieftains of Samoa and to the other small nations of the South Seas for which he had such affection:

"I will tell you, Chiefs, that, when I saw you working on that road, my heart grew warm, not with gratitude only, but with hope. It seemed to me that I read the promise of something good for Samoa; it seemed to me, as I looked at you, that you were a company of warriors in a battle, fighting for the defence of our common country against all aggression. For there is a time to fight, and a time to dig. You Samoans may fight, you may conquer twenty times, and thirty times, and all will be in vain. There is but one way to defend Samoa. Hear it before it is too late. It is to make roads, and gardens, and care for your trees, and sell their produce wisely, and, in one word, to occupy and use your country. If you do not, others will."

He spoke with grief of Hawaii, the sister country of Samoa, of how it had been depopulated and fallen into the hands of the white invaders; he told them about the Highlands in his own Scottish homeland, which had never recovered their former prosperity after being laid waste by so many foreign and civil wars.

243

"Now is the time for the true champions of Samoa to stand forth. And who is the true champion of Samoa? It is not the man who blackens his face, and cuts down trees, and kills pigs and wounded men. It is the man who makes roads, who plants food trees, who gathers harvests, and is a profitable servant before the Lord, using and improving that great talent that has been given him in trust. That is the brave soldier; that is the true champion. . . ."

It was inevitable that this European, who was preaching the European doctrine of hard work and productiveness out here in the Antipodes, should mention the great road builders, the Romans. Nor did he neglect to speak with love and loyalty of the man who was absent but of whom they were all thinking, Mataafa. Tusitala praised him both as an undaunted hero in battle and as one who had worked for the peaceful arts of farming and trade. ". . . when we turn our minds to the same matters, we may tell ourselves that we are still obeying Mataafa."

In the concluding words of his address to the Samoans, there was a sense of eternal values. The Romans, he said, had built roads in Europe which had lasted for more than a thousand years. The new road to Vailima was hardly built to last so long but, once built, roads have a strange vitality of their own; they collect people who use and repair and keep them alive. This new way would live "hundreds and hundreds of years after we are mingled in the dust."

At the end of so much serious talk about life and death,

there was a tremendous Samoan feast, gargantuan and joyful. They all sat on the floor of the long veranda; even the Europeans had no chairs, and there was not even a table to groan under the weight of the food. The courses were served to the squatting guests in little baskets and on leaves, and there was no sign of a fork anywhere to be seen. They ate all the good things of Samoa, pig, roasted in a pit in the ground, and coconut pudding wrapped in taro leaves; but they were also provided with their favourite European delicacies, corned beef, canned salmon and hardtack. Eighty great pineapples were consumed, and grapes, too. Then the guests who were present carried out the Samoan custom of packing up whatever was left over to take home. A High Chief dance of pantomimic character called a Siva, was executed with great solemnity on the lawn in front of the house. Then the festival of thanksgiving came to an end.

The great celebration in honour of the opening of the "Road of the Loving Hearts" was hardly over when another anniversary came round to be marked. Towards the end of 1894, the household in Vailima was in a particularly holiday mood. Stevenson's birthday (now Anne-Louise Ide's) fell on November 11; he was forty-four years old on that day.

Then, at the end of the month, there was Thanksgiving Day, with a big turkey dinner, celebrated in the fashion of the Pilgrim Fathers of Fanny's homeland. Could this day have passed without a real banquet around the old mahogany table, with star-spangled flags, and all the American colony as guests? They even had all the traditional dishes of an American Thanksgiving dinner. Fanny, the super chef, had hunted up something which looked like a cranberry, even if it did not taste like it—a small red berry, native to the Samoan woods. The other trimmings included sweet potato pudding, and real American apples, which had arrived by steamer the day before. Before the meal they had real cocktails. When Talolo brought in the champagne in a wine cooler with real ice with the dessert course, the general level of enthusiasm was raised to the highest point. Judge Mulligan, the new American consul-general, stood up before the table glittering with silver and crystal, and made a speech which was both witty and patriotic, in honour of Tusitala's hospitable house and of the American national holiday.

Stevenson did not listen; his thoughts were on the fate of young Archie Hermiston. All of these parties were delaying his work and he was inwardly impatient, although his weak and playful nature impelled him to give in to the general mania of holiday making. The applause which followed the consul-general's remarks roused him from his none too festive reflections. He stood up quickly to express his thanks to the consul and to say, in an adequate way, how much he owed to America. He looked around the table at the assembled guests. They were all Americans, as were also his wife and his stepchildren. The only American who was missing was Moors, the man who had wanted to carry him off to Nassau, away from the American part of his double life, away from Fanny. Moors had gone away again on a journey.

Stevenson's speech of gratitude was confined, as it should be on Thanksgiving Day, to America, to which he owed his fame and success in even greater measure than to his own country. He spoke also of his wife, whom he owed to America.

Fanny sat there, her face dark with emotion which she could hardly keep under control. Stevenson's old mother began to sob when he spoke of her in a way dear to the hearts of the Americans, and made some appropriate remarks about how thankful he was that he still had her and that he could have her near him.

Then he saw Lloyd sitting there silent with his eyes on his plate, so he mentioned him, as well as Belle, in an affectionate way, saying that he looked upon them as his children. And when little Austin Strong smiled at him from the other end of the table he smiled back to him and said:

"Vailima is blessed, for there is a child in the house."

And they all drank a toast to American women.

CHAPTER XVI

GOD'S FRAGMENTS

THE giving of thanks knew no end. "We thank Thee and we praise Thee," was the prayer said on the Sunday after Thanksgiving Day by Stevenson. His family and his Samoan household listened with devout attention as he prayed: "We beseech Thee, Lord, to behold us with favour. . . . Be patient still; suffer us yet a while longer;—with our broken purposes of good, and our idle endeavours against evil—suffer us awhile longer to endure, and (if it may be) help us to do better. Bless to us our extraordinary mercies; if the day come when these must be taken, have us play the man under affliction. Be with our friends, be with ourselves. Go with each of us to rest; if any awake, temper to them the dark hours of watching; and when the day returns, return to us, our sun and comforter, and call us up with morning faces and with morning hearts—eager to labour—eager to be happy, if happiness be our portion—and if the day be marked for sorrow, strong to endure it."

The little community said the Lord's Prayer. "Thy will be done. . . . Forgive us our debts. . . . Deliver us from evil." But there was no entreaty to be delivered from death.

The great and wise Author of the Lord's Prayer had not taught men to ask for anything so foolish.

There were indeed grounds enough for thanksgiving. Robert Louis Stevenson had just turned forty-four and felt younger than ever; he was full of a youthfulness that was infinitely more fresh, more manly than it had ever been. For the first time in many years he seemed to be in almost complete possession of all of his powers. He could tell from his mother's eyes how healthy he had grown. He seemed to have reached a turning point in his life as a writer, as Tusitala, as a Prospero on a tropical isle, when everything was shaping itself for good, for peace and for completion. He had stopped work on his second-rate book *St. Ives,* whose only purpose was to entertain, and was devoting all of his great energy to his future masterpiece, *Weir of Hermiston.* But since he always felt the need of keeping several manuscripts on the stocks at once, he took up once more the unfinished piece about his own family, *A Family of Engineers.* He could not prove that they derived from the MacGregors, but it was a favourite dream of his that the Stevensons were kin to the Highland rebel Rob Roy. Then came a line of generations of lighthouse engineers, who had built lifesaving towers of light along the stormy northern coasts of Scotland. There was Robert Louis Stevenson's grandfather, and Thomas, his own father, and he himself had been destined to the same career only to turn into something so completely different. Perhaps he had been impelled to write this autobiography by the same motives which move many writers towards the end of their lives. Perhaps he wanted to prove the completion of the circle, the revolving light which swung from Rob Roy to the author of *Kidnapped.* In the annals of this pious and matter-of-fact family of engineers, there were few traces of Highland romance, but R. L. S. was convinced that they must exist, and that they had come down to his generation from his remote Celtic ancestors. He was just as positive that his passionate love of the sea, islands and cliffs, was a direct inheritance from his lighthouse-building ancestors. Perhaps he might have followed the history of the Stevenson engineers with the story of his own life; but even that book was never finished.

Nothing was finished in those days which followed his forty-fourth birthday. Everything pressed for completion, for polishing, for final summing up, or, according to the point of view, for a marshalling of forces for a fresh start. After all the years during which this castaway Scot in the South Seas had longed in vain to see his old friends, a letter arrived at last from one of his oldest and most intimate friends: Charles Baxter, fellow traveller on some of his first journeys, a comrade of his student days, was actually on his way to Samoa! He could hardly believe it. Sidney Colvin was not coming; no, he just continued to write severe letters to his friend in exile, and complained of hearing too much from R. L. S. about his "blacks and his chocolates," the people of Samoa with whom, after all, Stevenson had to live. Colvin would continue to sit in the British Museum in London, but, oh joy! Charlie was coming. They would be able to show him Vailima, the island of Upolu, all of Samoa, the whole of the microcosm of which his banished friend had become master and king. If only for a few weeks he would join in the charming game of "Tusitala," just as, long ago, he had been part of the venturesome canoe expeditions Stevenson undertook through the firths and lakes of Scotland. He would have his friend there, and they could take up and go on with their interrupted youth. Louis would be able to show Charlie his "blacks and chocolates" at close range. Perhaps he could then go back and explain to that stubborn Colvin why it was that these people were interesting and important, and why R. L. S. had been forced to become a Prospero in the South Seas, and how he had nevertheless succeeded, as Shakespeare's Prospero had done, in making his life in banishment into something worth while for himself and a blessing for others. . . .

Another almost more important cause for rejoicing than the imminent arrival of his friend was the thing that Charles Baxter had promised to bring with him: the first volume of the Edinburgh Edition of the Collected Works of Robert Louis Stevenson.

It had long been his wish to see his works collected in some enduring form such as this Edinburgh Edition, for he was quite prepared for the eventuality of dying young. But could they be in enduring form so long as they did not include the finished novel, *Weir of Hermiston?* He felt that as long as that was lacking, there could be nothing final, nothing lasting in quality about the collection. To be sure, the many volumes would include all of his romantic stories of adventure, charming travel sketches, pretty rhymes, but they would only serve more or less as a prologue to his one important piece of writing. This he was now in the process of creating, and chapter by chapter he was forging ahead. Perhaps there would be novels later on on this same new high level, perhaps *The Young Chevalier* would attain it, and in the series of South Sea stories his great book *Sophia Scarlet.* But all of that was still on the knees of the gods, whereas he could surely finish *Weir of Hermiston* before the fleet phantom steed, whose hoofs he heard so distinctly on the day of the paper chase and whose image had been in his mind ever since, would overtake him.

During these days Lloyd Osbourne often saw his step-father, who was now so healthy and full of life, look up to the crest of Mt. Vaea as though he were trying to measure the distance up there. He did it every morning when he worked with utmost concentration with Belle, dictating one more bit of *Weir of Hermiston.* He did it every evening as he dressed himself in a fresh white suit and gay coloured sash, for some social function. Then the high top of his mountain of destiny was still to be seen in the glow of the sunset.

But in the tropics night falls quickly.

Meanwhile life went on. There were happy gatherings and sad good-byes. To the great regret of the household of Vailima, the *Curaçao* was ordered away and steamed off after many farewell toasts, many renderings of *Auld Lang Syne* and many "Auf Wiedersehens." After they had left, another British war vessel, *H.M.S. Wallaroo,* came to Samoa. On their very first day there, three Scotsmen from the ship, with an unerring instinct, found the way out to Vailima. Then Fanua Gurr produced a charming baby, who naturally had to be christened. Also there was much to be talked over with young Count Festetics who was getting his yacht, the *Tolna,* ready to pursue its journey around the world.

One thing to be discussed had to do with the fact that Palema, Graham Balfour, who had gone off in October on an ethnographical study cruise to some far-flung islands, was to visit Mataafa in Jaluit and take him presents and greetings from Tusitala. Yet was that really the whole extent of his purpose? Had he not been entrusted with some secret mission by Tusitala?

Afterwards, Count Festetics stated, in his none too reliable accounts of his travels, that he had made an agreement with Stevenson to turn the adventurous course of his yacht in the direction of the Marshall Islands, to free Mataafa, and bring him back to Samoa, where his appearance at this juncture would surely result in chasing Laupepa off his throne, or rather off his ancestral mat.

In the last conversations which took place between Steven-

253

son and the enterprising young Hungarian Count, they at least mentioned the possibility of carrying out this highly adventurous plan. Whereas everything else in Tusitala's life was being shaped for a rounding up, a balancing of accounts, a conclusion, in this project lay the seeds of a brand-new adventure, perhaps of new complications. As long as there is life in a man, he wants to put out new shoots, fresh buds.

But on the tree of life not all the buds come out.

Whatever may have been the playful plans for branching out into new activities, there was really only one dominating interest in Robert Louis Stevenson's life during the latter part of 1894: this was the urge to go on with his manuscript of *Weir of Hermiston.* They talked about it a great deal in the family, but except for Belle, to whom he dictated several pages each day, no one had seen so much as a single line of it. Finally Louis' mother and Fanny grew impatient and begged him to read them the chapters he had already completed. For a few days he seemed to be opposed to this idea, and then suddenly he gave in. One evening at the very end of November he gathered the family together and read aloud to them, making a pause at the end of each of the short chapters. Each time, the ladies broke into almost excessive applause. But Lloyd Osbourne sat silent in his corner. A sheet of blank paper lay before him. He had intended to make notes on it, but he never even took up his pencil, and he did not utter a single word. As he was reading, R. L. S. often threw a brief but sharp look in his direction.

When he had finished reading, Stevenson laid his papers down in silence. He made hardly any reply to the enthusiastic praise and inquiries of the women. Lloyd Osbourne got up, poured himself a whiskey and soda which he gulped down, and then, with a curt good night he left the house to go home to his cottage under the coco palms.

Just as he reached the garden gate and was about to close it, his stepfather caught up with him. His eyes flashed through the dark. He grabbed Lloyd's arm with surprising vigour, his thin fingers dug into the flesh, as he shouted:

"Good God, you are not going to leave me like *that*! You have not said one word to me, not one single word. You haven't even the decency to pretend to like my book! You are the only person here on whose judgment I can rely, and all you say is 'Good night, Louis!' and go away. 'Good night, Louis' indeed! Why didn't you strike me a blow in the face and be done with it?"

He haled his unwilling stepson back into the hall. The women had gone off to bed; perhaps their womanly instincts had made them feel that an explanation was about to take place and they cleared the field.

The big lamp went out. The two men stood facing each other in the dark. No one could see how pale young Lloyd was. He was trembling all over, and his glasses were blurred by the cold perspiration that broke out over his entire body. He wanted to speak, but could not bring out a single word. He had wanted to speak for a long time, but he had never been able to do it. Even now he was in the grip of some inexplicable inhibition. For a moment the obstacle appeared to be insuperable; between him and this raging man there was a wall of stone which was both impenetrable and cold. But in the next moment, without any warning, that wall suddenly melted away—it had vanished and out from his inner soul there poured a torrent of warm words.

"Louis," he said, "in my opinion no finer pages have ever been written in the English language than your *Weir of Hermiston*. It is your masterpiece; it will be your high-water mark. Forgive me: I wanted to say this long ago, but I just could not put it into words."

He reached out in the dark for his stepfather's hand.

After that, everything was smoothed out between them. Here was another circle which was rounded out. Robert Louis Stevenson felt that here he had close to him once more the boy to whom he had told the story of the treasure island. Now, as then, they heard the patter of a heavy rain as they sat together in the darkness of the night in the hall of Vailima. They both thought of that rainy afternoon in the Scottish Highlands, but neither of them spoke of it.

They sat together in the damp darkness; they could not see each other, and because of that they could speak more freely, with less embarrassment, without their daytime restraints. Lloyd could feel that the arm around his shoulders was trembling. And in the vibrant voice he knew so well, he sensed the invisible tears which were coursing down Louis' face.

In this hour Stevenson said things that he had never told to anyone before; about how deeply he had suffered under his physical disability, how he felt like a cripple, how his illness gave him a sense of being disgraced by some crime.

"It is not the discomfort I have felt all my life, Lloyd; it is the degradation, the physical shame of not being a healthy person among others who are. . . ."

That I should have been thinking of leaving him! was the thought in Lloyd's mind. He gave no utterance to it, but he was deeply moved. I had thought of going away, of taking the offer of that American publishing house.

The man sitting beside him was so close to him now that he immediately guessed his thoughts.

"No, do not leave me," said Robert Louis Stevenson. "It will not be long now."

And as he felt his son tremble under his arm he added: "No, no! Now I want to live again. But believe me, I have often enough longed for death. But now I want to live on, Lloyd."

That night Stevenson was so excited that it was long before he could get to sleep, and when he finally did drop off he had a lively and colourful dream.

He was a boy once more, and his beloved nurse "Cummy" had him recite a poem; it was really the same difficult poem that little Austin had to say for Aunt Maggie's birthday, but the boy Louis could not pronounce the long, complicated words. He made a bow to Cummy—no, it was Aunt Maggie now, and he wanted to recite the verses to her, but an entirely different poem came from his lips, one he had written long ago in California, when he was so very ill and thought that he must die:

"Requiem," said the boy Louis in his dream, and he made another bow. Then he went on:

> "Under the wide and starry sky,
>   Dig the grave and let me lie.
> Glad did I live and gladly die,
>   And I laid me down with a will.
>
> "This be the verse you grave for me
>   *Here he lies where he longed to be;*
> *Home is the sailor, home from sea,*
>   *And the hunter home from the hill."*

The boy Louis, who was also the boy Austin as well as the boy Lloyd, wanted to make a proper bow at the end of his recitation to Cummy, his old nurse—who in some strange way was also his mother Margaret Stevenson and Austin's Aunt Maggie—but he found himself unable to do it. He was no longer a civilized little boy, but that impertinent young savage Soolevao, and yet, in some unaccountable way, he was Robert Louis Stevenson, that writer with an impish expression on his face whom R. L. S. had often seen in the mirror. Now he was speaking to his mother, who was also God, in a rather sharp voice and saying: "Who made God anyway?"

With a terrific racket a huge boulder crashed down from the top of Mt. Vaea, right into the bedroom, and rolled slowly onto the sleeping man's frail chest. R. L. S. sobbed in his sleep. Then Long John Silver, that terrible pirate of *Treasure Island,* the ship's cook with a wooden leg, attacked him. No, it was someone else, an unknown man. It was terrifying; he could not guess, R. L. S. could not guess, who it was who was tearing at his chest.

He screamed: "Cummy!" and his own cry wakened him.

But he fell asleep again at once. He was so tired that he felt his body sink into his bed and become one with it. Now he no longer saw changing dream figures. He began to think in his dreams, and his thoughts were clearer than they had ever been during all his life.

—God also invented the little boy Soolevao, thought the sleeping novelist's brain. This pert little fellow is also something God has written. Every human being is a character in a novel by God. The Divine Poet sometimes rounds out a whole story with a beginning, a middle and an end; he invents thousands and thousands of little episodes in all of their details. But some of his creations are merely notes or sketches; the trend of the action is there, but the hero's profile is not well defined.

And sometimes—this was clear to the sleeping man—

259

sometimes God tucks a story he has begun away again; He will come back to it some day, and finish it. Yes, some day! For God has a special love for these fragments; they are important to Him. . . .

"For you know, Ernest," said the dreamer to Henley, the long-lost friend of his youth, who was suddenly quite close to him again, so that he could confide his most important and best thoughts to him; "for you know, Ernest, God's fragments are far from being His worst creations. In fact, they are usually better than the lengthy novels full of plot which He writes out to the end. Nearly every ending to a novel is somehow tiresome and banal, don't you think so, Ernest? But there is no end to a fragment; it goes on as it is, until one day God will take it out of His great writing case and finish it. . . .

This thought made Stevenson quite happy, so happy that he began to smile in his dream. And he smiled himself over into a deep and dreamless sleep.

CHAPTER XVII

A WILFUL CONVULSION OF BRUTE NATURE

EARLY in the morning of December 3, 1894, Stevenson woke up with a distinct sense of well-being. He drank with relish the cup of tea brought to him in his bedroom by the sleepy Sosimo, smoked his first cigarette while still in bed and then set to work. Which meant that he drew up his legs and rested his notebook against his knees. In this way he half-sat and half-lay in bed, making notes in preparation for the pages he would dictate later on in the day to Belle. He was just at the beginning of the ninth chapter of *Weir of Hermiston,* which was to include an important scene between the two lovers. R. L. S. could visualize it quite clearly:

It is in the afternoon; the last rays of the setting sun shine through a cleft in the mountain chain and illumine the lonely "Stone of the Praying Weaver," where Archie and Kirstie have met. The girl, who is completely absorbed in her tender love, waits for her beloved. But today he comes to her with a heavy heart and a grim face.

R. L. S. made a note of what Archie would say when Kirstie opened her arms to him.

261

"No, Christina, not to-day. To-day I have to talk to you seriously. Sit ye down, please, there where you were. Please!" The two figures moved gracefully in his mind's eye; the scene was full of life already, and would develop by itself. When Kirstie's aunt had appealed to the conscience of this decent but weak young man, he had given her a promise. Besides, his friend Frank, who is the Mephistopheles of this little tragedy, has, for reasons of his own, whispered things into his ear. So now Archie comes to this girl, whom he loves and who loves him, with the best intentions in the world, to preach her a wise sermon.

R. L. S. jotted down quickly, with his illegible handwriting, a good sentence which had just occurred to him:

"The schoolmaster that there is in all men, to the despair of all girls and most women, was now completely in possession of Archie. . . ."

Yes, that was the idea; under the pretext of giving prudent counsel, Archie began to lecture his beloved most unmercifully. He told her that they must not meet so often, and that especially they must not be seen together so much, that people are already beginning to talk about them.

The pencil wrote in the notebook: "The first thing that we must see to, is that there shall be no scandal about for my father's sake. That would ruin all; do ye no see that?"

There it was; the shadow of the other Weir of Hermiston, of the severe father, which was to fall between the two lovers. That would be enough to offend a proud girl like Kirstie, to drive her into a state of resentment. All that he needs to do is to bring the hated name of his false friend into the discussion and the estrangement would be complete.

His pencil flew over the paper. Stevenson hastily added several sentences for Kirstie, in broad Scotch:

". . . Little wonder if a'body's talking, when ye make a'body ye're confidants! . . . I have naething to do with it. And I think I'll better be going. I'll be wishing you good evening, Mr. Weir."

And below that he put: "She drops him a formal curtsey."

R. L. S. grinned to himself as he sat there in bed. That was the right setting for a scene between two people who are fond of each other. Archie will of course soften again at once. But it will be too late; the estrangement, this brief thunderstorm, is necessary in order to introduce the subsequent tragic turn of events into this little idyll.

Stevenson laid aside his notebook and decided that he would get up shortly. He was all impatience to dictate these pages before the flood of his ideas was checked again.

He came downstairs in a good humour. He saw Fanny out in the garden and joined her. In the garden it smelled of orange blossoms; the frangipani trees were laden with white flowers shaped like trumpets, which exhaled their melodies instead of blowing them. The gardenias were still shining with dew. In the early morning a tropical garden can look incredibly fresh and almost as trim as a garden in the north.

But Fanny's face looked like a black tropical thundercloud. She hardly returned her husband's cheerful greeting and was full of irritable complaints. She had slept badly; she felt oppressed and nervous. "You'll see, Lou," she said, "we shall have some bad news. Probably from Graham. We should never have let him go off again in that rickety boat among those dangerous atolls."

"Oh, nothing will happen to him," said R. L. S. cheerfully. "He's a bad penny who will always return. And the schooner he is on this time is not half bad."

"Provided he doesn't do anything foolish in Jaluit," Fanny persisted. "You'll see. I am always right when I have these premonitions of trouble."

"Nonsense," said Louis, who by this time was a little upset himself.

Lloyd strolled by, dressed for a ride. After his talk with his stepfather, he looked quite different, much happier, even better in health. He said that he had to hurry into town, and would probably be back just in time for lunch. As he went by, Louis gave him a little comradely slap on the back and, pretending to be a careworn father, he warned him against hanging around the bars in Apia until he was half-seas over.

Then he turned to Isobel, who had just made her appearance, all dressed in white. "Well, Sleepyhead, is this the way for a zealous secretary to behave herself? We must get to work, my child, to work!"

264

He chased her into the study much as a goosegirl might shoo her feathered charges. She ran laughingly ahead of him, but as she went she threw a backward glance at Fanny, who was stooping unnecessarily low over a gardenia bush and hiding her clouded face.

Stevenson's study was arranged for work and was furnished with extreme simplicity. A thick curtain hung over the greater part of the entrance to dull the sounds inside and to prevent noise breaking in from the outside. There were bookshelves made out of a few planks along one wall, and on them were scattered a scanty assortment of books—they were in the wilds of Samoa—in a rather disorderly arrangement. It looked like the library of a man who doesn't keep his books to show their bindings. These shelves filled the space to the left of the door, and in that corner R. L. S. had a chair which he used more to jump up out of than to sit in. It was an ordinary, uncomfortable wooden chair. On the walls there were a few pictures, mostly prints of Scottish landscapes, and two great pistols, trophies which looked dangerous but were hardly usable. On a ledge there were a water jug and various odds and ends of bric-a-brac. To the right of the door his secretary Belle had a low stool, on which she sat, holding a large writing case across her knees while she wrote. Beyond this there was little in the room except for a few small letter files and similar trifles.

When R .L. S. and Belle came into this room, they adopted

a more formal attitude towards each other, as they sat down, the one on the upholstered stool near the door, the other on the hard wooden chair. He jumped up again almost immediately and turned his chair so that he could watch Isobel as she wrote. He stood with his left hand on the back of his chair, balancing the upper part of his body on it. This looked somewhat precarious, especially as he never stayed still for more than a moment and kept teetering the chair back and forth until it was in imminent danger of tipping over.

Today he was dressed only in a pair of trousers, a loose shirt open at the neck, and one of his romantic, gay coloured sashes.

He was in particularly good form. The chapter he planned to dictate was as distinct in his mind as an open road before a traveller. The preparatory work he had done earlier in the morning had cleared away all obstacles. He glanced briefly now and then into his notebook, and that was sufficient to help him to establish the exact formulation of a sentence. But one could not really say that R. L. S. dictated the text of his novel; it was rather the living, self-willed people in his novel who dictated the text to him. Now he came to poor Kirstie's great outbreak of temper.

" 'Kirstie, indeed!' cried the girl, her eyes blazing in her white face. 'My name is Miss Christina Elliott, I would have ye to ken, and I daur ye to ca' me out of it. If I canna get love, I'll have respect, Mr. Weir. I'm come of decent people, and I'll have respect. What have I done that ye should lightly me? What have I done? What have I done? O, what have I done?' and her voice rose upon the third repetition. 'I thocht—I thocht—I thocht I was sae happy!' and the first sob broke from her like the paroxysm of some mortal sickness."

R. L. S. paused for a moment in his dictation. To tell the truth, this rift between the two lovers brought back to his mind the little scene between him and Fanny just before this down in the garden. When she had an attack of this sort of nervous depression, based on unfounded fears, or ruffled moods, he really ought to try to understand it better and be nice to her, and not just get up and go away. He forced himself to go on with the dictation, but it did not come so easily now.

"Archie ran to her. He took the poor child in his arms, and she nestled to his breast as to a mother's, and clasped him in hands that were strong like vices. He felt her whole body shaken by the throes of distress, and had pity upon her beyond speech. Pity, and at the same time a bewildered fear of this explosive engine in his arms, whose works he did not understand, and yet had been tampering with. There arose from before him the curtains of boyhood, and he saw for the first time the ambiguous face of woman as she is. In vain he looked back over the interview; he saw not where he had offended. It seemed unprovoked, a wilful convulsion of brute nature. . . ."

These were not the words that he had planned when in

bed; these words which he was dictating had more to do with Fanny than with Kirstie.

He made one further attempt to go on with the dictation. "Have you that, Belle?" And he repeated:

"It seemed unprovoked, a wilful convulsion of brute nature. . . ."

"Let's stop for today," said Stevenson suddenly. "I want to go and see what Fanny is doing."

Belle Strong had been sitting there like a bronze statue; in fact one might have inscribed on the base of her pedestal: "Portrait of a Zealous Secretary." Now she gave a knowing look. She was not a woman for nothing, and she had realized that in the last words of his dictation Louis was painting the little scene he had had with her mother. It had not been a quarrel; it was only a momentary expression of bad humour, but Fanny's husband could not quiet down until he had made up to her for having needlessly rubbed her the wrong way.

So the dictation of *Weir of Hermiston* was cut off short, on the third page of the ninth chapter, right in the middle of a sentence, and just after the words, "a wilful convulsion of brute nature."

The process of consoling Fanny took all of Stevenson's time up to luncheon, and then he frittered away the whole afternoon in childish pranks of one kind or another. He did that sometimes. He up and announced that he was a "chattering little idiot boy"—and proceeded to behave himself in character. These were the days when his puckishness was rampant; he was full of restlessness and comic little tricks. He would draw pictures of funny little men, or tell Scotch jokes, imitating Harry Lauder, or else he would tease everyone who came near him. When Lloyd came back from town, hot and tired, he met him in the garden and made a long parody of a congratulatory speech in praise of his marvellous efficiency as chief overseer of the plantation of Vailima. Before he had gone into town, Lloyd had left orders for some of the native boys to mow the grass on the tennis court. They had done it very neatly except that in some places they had left the tall blades standing, and on examination one could make out that they represented Lloyd's name in Samoan, Loia, and it was intended as a delicate compliment to him. But of course it was impossible to play tennis on the lawn. R. L. S. pretended that Lloyd had had the whole thing done out of conceit, and there was no end to the jokes he made on the subject. Lloyd did not lose his temper in the least (he was to remember that afterwards and be deeply happy that he had not been the least bit annoyed), but went on, laughing and whistling, over to his cottage. But before changing his clothes he thought he would take a dip in the pool.

Aunt Maggie, who saw her Lou so radiant with happiness, busied herself contentedly with some fancywork. Whereupon Louis went over to her and tried to see if he could crochet. Everyone laughed at his purposely exaggerated awkwardness. Only Fanny remained in a dark mood and finally said that she would have to go and attend to supper.

Stevenson followed her. Talolo's famous kitchen shone with cleanliness, and an excellent meal was almost ready. R. L. S. pretended to be obliged to inspect Talolo's work and he stuck his nose into every pot; he was still full of all kinds of playful exuberance.

He felt no shade of any premonition, whatever might be in Fanny's heart or clouded face. Not one single look out of the window to the crest of Mt. Vaea, around which the evening mists were gathering.

As Fanny prepared to help Talolo get the salad ready Louis said:

"Shall I make some mayonnaise for the salad? I can do it a great deal better than our great lady cook!"

He had begun to mix the oil with the condiments and was bending busily over the salad bowl, a mischievous boy.

For a moment there was a complete silence in the kitchen. Then suddenly they heard Robert Louis Stevenson's voice, which without any warning, had changed completely, terrifyingly. He said:

"Fanny, how do I look? Do I look strange?"

That was the last question of a man who never during his whole life, and for all his nonchalant posing, had been indifferent to his own appearance and to its effect on other people.

Fanny looked at him and replied, with the comforting tone

270

of a mother: "You seem as usual, Lou!" It was a brave lie, for he was ghastly pale, and she knew at once that it was the pallor of death.

He swayed and was about to fall. Fanny was just able, with the help of the faithful Talolo, to get him into the great hall where he was laid in his beloved big armchair. He was still alive, in a certain sense, but the light in those wonderful eyes which had made the world of his day a little brighter, that light was gone forever. Apparently without sense and for no reason a "wilful convulsion of brute nature" had brought the life of Robert Louis Stevenson to a close. And with his dying brain, there also died the unfulfilled figures of his last great novel, Kirstie Elliott and Weir of Hermiston.

CHAPTER XVIII

UNDER THE WIDE AND STARRY SKY

THE members of the household gathered together, some sobbing and others stunned with grief. When his mother reached the hall, he was unconscious, but faintly groaning. Lloyd Osbourne, with the tears coursing down his cheeks, saddled his horse. It was the thoroughbred, Saumai Afe, the horse he had ridden on the paper chase, behind R. L. S. He had won many races with this horse, but he did not win this one. He made better time along the "Road of the Loving Hearts" today than on that morning when Stevenson had introduced himself as Mr. Dumbley. He went straight to the little German physician, Dr. Funk, who with his full grey beard looked like Admiral von Tirpitz. He tore him reluctantly from his evening meal, almost using force to get him to mount the race horse Saumai Afe and gallop off. The doctor was terrified by the animal's wildness and only did as Lloyd wished after the latter had taken charge of his medical kit; he needed both hands to cling to the saddle. With the doctor's bag in his hand, and the bottles and instruments rattling around in it, Lloyd Osbourne ran through the dark streets of the little colonial town. Somewhere he found a horse tied to a fence. He asked no questions, jumped on his back and soon overtook the old doctor who, groaning and sighing, was bouncing along the road.

The doctor from His Majesty's ship *Wallaroo,* which had replaced the *Curaçao,* was quickly reached, and followed them to Vailima.

At Robert Louis Stevenson's bedside these two representatives of medical science had no help to offer, only some learned theories. One of them said a blood vessel had probably burst in the brain; the other used the expression embolism and stated that it sometimes happened, with tubercular patients, that an infected particle broke loose from some cavity and clogged a vessel in the brain.

All trace of the irony and impishness, which had been so much a part of the dead man's expressive features, was gone now; he looked serene and solemn.

Tusitala was laid on a bier in his much beloved great hall. His body was dressed in festive attire; there were patent leather shoes on his feet and his legs were encased in the trousers of his dress clothes. He had no coat on, and a dark blue sash was wound around his body. He was dressed in a soft white shirt, on which was pinned the little silver thistle brooch, the emblem of the Thistle Club of Honolulu, which Stevenson had worn ever since his return from Hawaii; it lay over his Scottish heart.

He looked as he would have wished to on his bier; dignified and at the same time picturesque. He loved to go barefoot, but he was attached to his patent leather shoes too, and they emphasized the delicate shape of his feet.

On his finger was a simple silver wedding ring. When Stevenson had married Fanny, he could not afford a gold ring. They left the ring on his hand. Over the lower part of his body and his feet they laid the British Union Jack which, until then, had flown above the house; it had been the flag of the yacht *Casco,* on which R. L. S. made his great cruise among the South Sea Islands.

So he lay on his bier, with folded hands.

The native servants came and asked if they might "make a church" for him. This was granted, and as most of the employees in Vailima were Catholics, prayers for Tusitala's soul were said by Samoan lips in the language of Rome.

The night watch by the bier was held by the truest of the true, Talolo and Sosimo.

Before Dr. Funk had left the bereaved house he had, as an official of the department of health, arranged that the burial must take place before three in the afternoon of the following day; they were in the tropics. Lloyd Osbourne, in the midst of his terrible anguish, remembered with horror that the path which he had been supposed to build to the crest of the mountain did not yet exist; over and over again, under a thousand pretexts and compelled by some inner dread, he had avoided the construction of the way the sole purpose of

274

which was to lead more quickly and more easily to Louis' grave. And now what would happen? How could they carry a heavy coffin to the top of a steep mountain when there was no path?

The sad news of Tusitala's death had already spread with mysterious speed throughout the island. All through the night noiseless groups of dark-skinned men from neighbouring villages, High Chiefs and common folk, kept coming. They brought heavily scented tropical flowers and finely woven mats, which are held almost sacred by the Samoans and which are the heirlooms in the families of their princes. Their chieftains laid them respectfully on Tusitala's body until the flag of Britain was almost entirely hidden.

Every Samoan who came to the bier said: "Talofa, Tusitala," and kissed the pale face. Then they moved silently away. Some of them glanced timidly toward the iron strong box in the corner of the hall as if to make certain that the little imp had not escaped from his bottle.

Outside the Samoan mourners set immediately to work to build a last pathway for their beloved dead one. The same chieftains and their followers, who so recently and with so much joy had built the "Way of the Loving Hearts" for Tusitala, now used the same implements he had given them then, to hack a path through the bush and forest on the slopes of Mt. Vaea. All night long and through the morning hours the axes rang and the spades clanked. No path in Samoa was ever made so quickly; this Road of the Sorrowing Hearts was cut so swiftly that it almost seemed as though Aitu Fafine herself had lent her magic power to help its completion. By noon, a rough but passable trail was ready.

Meanwhile, in the town, Stevenson's good friend Clarke, the missionary, had undertaken the funeral arrangements, found a coffin, and invited guests to the service. But without waiting for any invitation, one Samoan chieftain after another arrived at Vailima; they came with flowers and mats; they stood in the hall a dozen paces from the dead man and spoke to him with all of their traditional and solemn ceremonial phrases, as though he were still alive and could hear them.

In the midst of their great and sincere grief, these speakers never were unconscious for a moment of the fact that they were standing by the body and the bier of a man whom they had put in the exalted rank of their own High Chiefs, and they never spoke a single word in the language one would use before the body of an ordinary man of the people.

This all proceeded so solemnly, so dramatically, that it would have taken the pen of Tusitala to give an accurate description of the many ceremonies. But Tusitala lay there silent and he was dead.

The house of Vailima did not even know some of the Samoans who had come to pay homage to Tusitala's bier. Suddenly a gigantic old chieftain had appeared in the centre of the hall; no one had ever seen him before or knew his name. Yet he must have been a High Chief of noble blood and some fine old race; that much was clear from his noble, firm carriage and his barbaric headdress. This savage old warrior of a bygone day spoke to Tusitala in ringing words which stirred everyone:

"Samoa comes to its end with you, Tusitala. When death sealed the eyes of our greatest and best friend we knew that the day of our people was drawing to its close."

Stevenson's funeral, in spite of the short time in which it had to be prepared, was as impressive as he undoubtedly would have wished it to be. Somehow they had succeeded in hastily procuring the traditional mourning clothes for all the servants of the household as well as for the whole clan of Tusitala—white loincloths and undershirts.

It was a frightfully sultry day; and they had to carry a heavy coffin up a roughly built trail through the virgin forest to the top of a high mountain. Relays of young warriors took turns as pallbearers; and they deemed it shameful to carry the beloved burden other than shoulder high. Slowly but steadily the coffin was swung along. The European mourners followed with difficulty, breathing heavily, losing their footing on the slippery layers of lava. Finally the mountain of death had been climbed, and they reached the little plateau on the crest of Mt. Vaea, which Stevenson himself had chosen to be his last resting place.

277

As the coffin was lowered into the grave, the minister pronounced, in clear tones, the Lord's Prayer:

"Thy Kingdom come, Thy will be done."

If those who were gathered at Tusitala's grave had looked down to the open sea, they might have been able to detect a faraway white object moving away from the island. It was the yacht *Tolna* leaving Samoa. Count Festetics de Tolna had learned of Stevenson's death just before his departure and had decided that under the tragic circumstances it would be better to give up the bold plan of abducting Mataafa from the island of Jaluit. Actually Mataafa was set free later without the intervention of force. After the Great Powers had finished carving up Samoa, and the greater part of the Archipelago had been made into a German colony, old Mataafa lived long and peaceably on the island of Upolu under the sage rule of the great governor Dr. Solf, who took up his residence then at Vailima. He was the most respected and ranked highest among all the High Chiefs of Samoa. Whenever his old friend Moors came to visit him, Mataafa always spoke with deep feeling of His Majesty Tusitala, of whom he and all of his fellow Samoans kept a faithful and grateful memory.

On the very day of the funeral the chieftains of the island of Upolu proclaimed one of their great tabus, which no Polynesian would dare to defy; and to this day none of the woodland birds, whose beautiful and mysterious calls had so often

278

delighted and frightened Tusitala on his walks, are allowed to be shot. They sing over his grave; and in the canoes or at work among the coco palms, the men and maidens of Samoa sing melancholy songs in honour of the white man who loved their island:

"Alas for Tusitala who reposes in the Forest! Without hope we wait. Will he never come again? Weep, o Vailima! To wait and ever to wait! Let us seek him everywhere, let us question the captains of ships: Do not be angry with us. Have you not Tusitala on board?"

It was not until 1914 that Robert Louis Stevenson's widow died, on her estate in California; in spite of being ten years his senior, and in spite of her delicate constitution, she outlived him by twenty years and reached a venerable age.

By that time Vailima no longer belonged to the family; yet Fanny's wish was carried out and she was buried beside Stevenson on the crest of Mt. Vaea, to the top of which all South Sea Island tourists climb.

Over them both lies a huge block of concrete in the form of a sarcophagus. There are plaques inlaid in the cement which bear the emblems of Scotland and Samoa, the thistle and the hibiscus flower. The tablet which bears Fanny's name has on it, in addition to the charming verses Stevenson once wrote about her, a design of a tiger lily. This is a perfect symbol for that passionate, strong, hot-blooded woman. On the memorial plaque for her husband, both of his names are inscribed: Robert Louis Stevenson and Tusitala. And of course there were added the words of the most beautiful requiem a poet ever composed for himself.

> "Under the wide and starry sky,
> Dig the grave and let me lie.
> Glad did I live and gladly die, . . ."

These words are like all the words of poets and perhaps of all human beings as well; they are both true and untrue; they are a mixture of belief and pose.

We are all glad to live, even those of us who are unhappy and ill; no one really dies gladly. Yet we shall be tired one day and long for rest as the sailor on the sea and the hunter in the depths of the forest. And hardly anyone of us believes that his life is so completely finished and rounded out that he can sincerely say: and glad I die.

Surely the poet Robert Louis Stevenson left his short and unfinished life too soon; of his last book only a fragment remains. This half-hewn block towers above all of his other charming works like a jagged peak above gentle foothills. So was his life, when he had to die; it was only an unfinished fragment which God took in its imperfect form and put away. But the Divine Poet loves the fragments he has created and one day, perhaps, He will finish them.

"Tales of the Pacific"

Journey into the watery world of atolls, roaring surf on coral reefs, blue lagoons, volcanoes and hurricanes, Polynesian kingdoms, and exotic brown women. Watch a cast of characters of beachcombers, whalers, missionaries, adventurers, traders, pearl hunters, mutineers, native chiefs, scientists, sun-hungry artists, and American G.I.'s. Read the best of the literature—fiction and nonfiction—from the earthly Paradises of the Pacific — the archipelagoes of Polynesia, Melanesia, and Micronesia. Enjoy dramatic narratives, short stories, and vignettes from a gallery of authors including Herman Melville, Mark Twain, Robert Louis Stevenson, Louis Becke, Jack London, W. Somerset Maugham, James Norman Hall, James Jones, Eugene Burdick, James A. Michener, and others that should be better known. Recall stirring adventures from the days of Captain James Cook and other early explorers through those of Pearl Harbor and the island-hopping campaigns of World War II!

These volumes of reprinted classics from Hawaii and the South Pacific are yours for only $3.95 each (unless otherwise noted). Editor of the series is Dr. A. Grove Day, Senior Professor, Emeritus, University of Hawaii, and author of histories and anthologies of the Pacific region.

To obtain a full description of "Tales of the Pacific" titles, write to Mutual Publishing, 2055 North King Street, Suite 201, Honolulu, Hawaii 96819. To order send $3.95 per book (add $1.00 handling fee for the first book, 50 cents thereafter). For further information or trade inquiries, call (808) 924-7732.

JACK LONDON

Stories of Hawaii
South Sea Tales
Captain David Grief (originally A Son of the Sun)
The Mutiny of the "Elsinore" ($4.95)

HAWAII

Remember Pearl Harbor by Blake Clark
Kona by Marjorie Sinclair
The Spell of Hawaii, ed. by A. Grove Day and Carl
    Stroven
A Hawaiian Reader, ed. by A. Grove Day and Carl
    Stroven
The Golden Cloak by Antoinette Withington
Russian Flag Over Hawaii by Darwin Teilhet
The Wild Wind by Marjorie Sinclair
Teller of Tales by Eric Knudsen
Myths and Legends of Hawaii by W.D. Westervelt, ed.
    by A. Grove Day

SOUTH SEAS LITERATURE

The Trembling of a Leaf by W. Somerset Maugham
Rogues of the South Seas by A. Grove Day
The Book of Puka-Puka by Robert Dean Frisbie
The Lure of Tahiti, ed. by A. Grove Day
The Blue of Capricorn by Eugene Burdick
Horror in Paradise: Grim and Uncanny Tales from
    Hawaii and The South Seas, ed. by A. Grove Day
    and Bacil F. Kirtley
Best South Sea Stories, ed. by A. Grove Day
The Forgotten One by James Norman Hall

TRAVEL, BIOGRAPHY, ANTHROPOLOGY

Manga Reva by Robert Lee Eskridge
Coronado's Quest: The Discovery of the American
    Southwest by A. Grove Day
Love in the South Seas by Bengt Danielsson
Road My Body Goes by Clifford Gessler
The House in the Rain Forest by Charis Crockett
My Tahiti by Robert Dean Frisbie
Home from the Sea: Robert Louis Stevenson in Samoa
    by Richard A. Bermann
The Nordhoff-Hall Story: In Search of Paradise by
    Paul L. Briand, Jr. ($4.95)